Dorset History
in 101 Objects

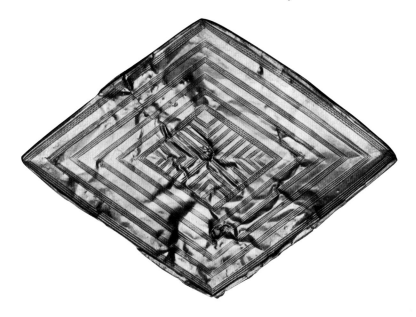

TERRY HEARING

DORSET BOOKS

First published in Great Britain in 2012

British Library Cataloguing-in-Publication Data
A CIP record for this title is available from the British Library

ISBN 978 1 871164 96 1

DORSET BOOKS
Dorset Books is a Partnership Between
Dorset County Council & Halsgrove

Halsgrove House,
Ryelands Business Park,
Bagley Road, Wellington, Somerset TA21 9PZ
Tel: 01823 653777   Fax: 01823 216796
email: sales@halsgrove.com

Part of the Halsgrove group of companies
Information on all Halsgrove titles is available at: www.halsgrove.com

Printed in China by Everbest Printing Co Ltd

Contents

Foreword

Mrs Anthony Pitt-Rivers
HM Lord-Lieutenant in Dorset

I AM DELIGHTED to introduce ' *Dorset History in 101 Objects*` by the well- known Dorset author Terry Hearing, who has lived in Martinstown near Dorchester for forty-six years and has written several books about the county he knows and loves.

For this new work he has made a personal and subjective study of objects, large and small, to illustrate and stimulate interest in our local history. His definition of the word `object` has many, sometimes unexpected, interpretations as he tells us about the bizarre and the beautiful, the famous and the obscure. Who would expect to find tiny Mesolithic microliths in the company of a Penny Farthing bicycle or Bournemouth Pier as a neighbour of St Wite`s shrine from Whitchurch Canonicorum?

Many of Terry Hearing`s favourites come from the Dorset History Centre, the County Museum and other local museums, but he also looks further afield and includes well-known landmarks such as Elisabeth Frink`s Martyrs Memorial in Dorchester, the Thornhill Obelisk and the Baden-Powell Memorial on Brownsea Island. Each short article gives his own view of an object and its importance in the continuing story of a county which is rich in the remains of the lives of our predecessors.

I am sure this book which celebrates Dorset`s past will encourage the reader to explore and seek out these and other treasures for themselves and remind us that the richness of our heritage is all around us if only we make time to look for it.

Acknowledgements

THE AUTHOR WOULD like to express his appreciation of the support he has received from many people in the preparation of this book, and in particular: Dr Jon Murden, Sam Johnston, George Wickham, Valerie Dicker, Peter Woodward, David Tucker, Steve Wallis, Ray Simpson, Jean Berry and Trevor Hearing.

Illustrations appear by courtesy of the following:

George Wickham, Dorset County Museum
pp 10, 13, 14, 16, 17, 19, 23, 24, 26, 27, 59, 69, 72, 73, 74, 75, 78, 79, 90, 100, 109, 119, 129, 131

Michael Spender, Poole Museum *pp 8, 11, 18, 104, 127*

Valerie Dicker, Dorset County Museum *pp 30, 31, 32, 84, 110, 115, 118, 121, 126*

Dorset History Centre *pp 39 (courtesy of Ilchester Estates), 50, 62, 105, 106, 133, 141*

David Allen/Stephen Lowy, Hampshire Arts and Museum Service HCC *pp 22, 35*

Emma Ayling/James Webb, The Priest's House Museum Collection Trust *pp 29, 79, 126*

David Tucker/Michael Applegate, Lyme Regis Museum *pp 70, 81, 92*

Ben Buxton, Wareham Museum *pp 40, 65*

Annabel Turner, Shaftesbury Abbey Museum and Gardens *pp 41, 47*

Emily Hicks, Bridport Museum Trust *pp 124, 125*

Capt. Colin Parr, The Keep Military Museum Dorchester *pp 87, 140*

Martin Langford, Bovington Tank Museum *pp 136, 137*

Trevor Hearing *p 120*

Dr Peter Andrews, Blandford Museum *p 113*

Andrew PM Wright, Swanage Railway *p 128*

Pauline Camm *p 135*

Ian Peterson, The Museum of Electricity, Christchurch *p 134*

All other colour photographs by the author

Introduction

THIS BOOK IS AN account of selected objects which illustrate the threads of the History of Dorset. The choice of objects was personal and subjective, and the author is aware that some readers will wonder why their own favourites have been left out – but that is inevitable. The definition of the word 'object' has been taken very widely, from the tiny Mesolithic microliths to the strip fields of Portland. Some of the objects are bizarre, such as the cannonball in the wall of a ladies' lavatory in Weymouth; some are very beautiful, like the Tabernacle in Milton Abbey; some are just names – the parish priests who died serving their flocks when the Black Death swept in.

Each short article attempts to give the flavour of the object and to show its importance in the continuing story of a county rich in the remains of the lives of our predecessors. All the objects are illustrated, but the originals can be seen in the museums, the towns and the countryside. It is hoped that the book will encourage exploration and research.

Dorset is fortunate in having a great variety of museums, as well as the Dorset History Centre, providing an enormous potential for the development of our understanding of the past. Planning for the future is likely to be much more successful when based on such understanding.

However, in the end we study History because it is interesting, and none is more interesting than that which we see around us and which is part of ourselves.

Terry Hearing

- 1 -
An Old Stone Age Hand Axe
Poole Museum

AT A CASUAL GLANCE it might seem just an ordinary lump of flint, of the sort to be seen in fields all over Dorset and across Britain. To the practised eye it is evidence of human culture: carefully shaped and finished to provide a vital tool – or a weapon. As such it is very significant, illustrating the lives of the first people of Dorset. Holding this piece of flint, a huge leap of imagination is needed to picture those lives.

Wandering across the country (still attached to the European land-mass), small groups gathered fruits, nuts and roots, and hunted. They followed the herds of wild cattle, picking off weak animals. Shelter was crude and temporary, unless convenient caves could be found. Fear must have dominated their lives, with multiple hazards at every turn. Life must have been indeed 'nasty, brutish and short'.

But people survived in this way for unimaginable millennia – hundreds of thousands of years. The earliest stone tools so far discovered in Dorset are more than 300,000 years old, but in Norfolk a handaxe reckoned to be 550,000 was found a few years ago. Climate changes frequently altered the geography of the area we know as Dorset. The retreat of the last Ice Age 10,000 years ago led to the rise in sea-level which created the islands of Britain. As the cliffs along the Dorset coast crumble they reveal more and more fossilised evidence of times far beyond the first human beings, of earth movements and land creations in a period known to geologists as the Jurassic. For our Stone Age ancestors the sea would have been a great barrier, but a valuable source of gatherable food.

For the everyday tasks of cutting wood, scraping animal skins, prising-open seashells – stone tools were essential. Specialist makers of tools used their skills to barter their produce for food – and trade developed. Archaeologists find tools far from the sources of flint.

Inevitably tools were also weapons, and competition for resources would have led to fighting, but the evidence is undiscovered, and we can only surmise. If you have the chance to handle a Stone Age hand axe, feel, and imagine its first owner.

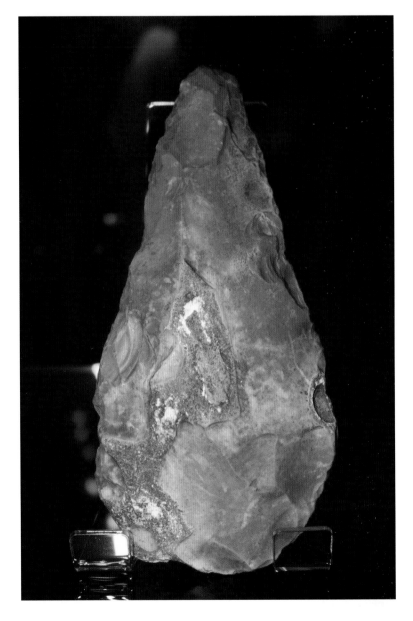

Flint Quarry.

Mesolithic Microliths
Dorset County Museum

IN THE IMMENSELY long time of humanoid activity known as Palaeolithic or the Old Stone Age, the periodic changes of climate, vegetation and sea-level had led to times when the north and west of Britain was covered in ice.

About 10,000 BC the temperature began to rise, the ice receded northwards, and the grass tundra gave way to woodland with a variety of trees. This meant different, smaller animals lived there and could be hunted – deer and boar, though the herds of wild oxen continued to roam.

The use of heavy stone axes chipped from flint nodules also continued, but by 8000 BC human beings had developed enough to make good use of the flakes of stone that had been chipped away. They could be fashioned by more careful chipping to form finer instruments for war and peace. Particularly, the sharpened chips could make arrowheads, spearheads, picks for extracting shell-fish and knives for cutting meat.

In the period known as Mesolithic (the Middle Stone Age – roughly 8000 to 4000 BC) people scattered their microliths or fine stone tools in sites across Dorset, but especially along river banks and in woodland clearings. Meantime, the sea rose and Britain had separated from the Continent. Dorset had a coastline.

Microliths
- carefully worked small tools
set as teeth in sickles, saws etc.
From Iwerne Minster

A Neolithic Pot
Poole Museum

AROUND 3000 BC a new people migrated into Britain, and brought with them technology that created a lifestyle that was new to the island.

Their stone implements and weapons were much more finely shaped, with wooden handles. This was still the Stone Age – they had no metal – but they planted crops, reared cattle and sheep, and made pottery. These are the elements of civilised life, in a culture which was far in advance of nomadic hunter-gathering.

Their settlements were not necessarily long-lived – without fertiliser the soil was exhausted after a few years, and new clearings in the woodland had to be made – but the essence of community is to be seen in what these Neolithic people left behind. Across Dorset are to be seen their tombs.

These are the 'long barrows': mounds of earth, hundreds of feet long, covered elaborate wooden burial-chambers. Where stone slabs were available they were used for the construction itself, as in 'The Grey Mare and her Colts' near Portesham. Circular earthworks known as 'henges' seem to have been religious sites.

Pottery is perhaps the most significant survival to indicate a more developed way of life. Pots meant storage, cooking-vessels and convenient drinking, and their manufacture could become industry and trade. Their decoration represented the higher culture of art. Civilisation was on its way.

Untamed Dorset.

A Neolithic Jade Axehead
Dorset County Museum

AT A TIME WHEN life for human beings was a desperate struggle for survival, it was still possible for someone to create an artefact whose beauty made it quite impossible to use.

The jade axehead found at Newton Peveril near Sturminster Marshall is one such object.

The axe is about 7 inches by 3 inches, and is dated to around 4000BC. The jade stone came from the Italian Alps, and it is likely that the long and painstaking process of grinding and polishing took place in Brittany. The creation was expensive in time and exotic in concept, and inspires many unanswerable questions. Why was it made? How did it come to Britain? What demand did it fulfil, other than the joy of possession?

The jade axehead is not unique. A similar one (though not quite so fine) was found at Canterbury in Kent, and tests have shown that it was taken from the same block of stone. At all events the artefact demonstrates that there was movement of people and goods across Europe at this time, that there was appreciation of beauty and that at least some people had enough wealth to afford to indulge that appreciation. Since the tool was never used – though it could have been – presumably it stood on the Stone Age equivalent of a sideboard, to be admired by friends, to be inherited, or to be presented as a special gift.

- 5 -
A Hoard of Bronze Axeheads
Dorset County Museum

If the people we call Neolithic created the beginnings of modern culture with their farming and pottery, it was their successors in the second millennium BC who, in the period known as the Bronze Age, really pressed ahead to develop metalwork and even to explore mathematics.

Metalworking came to Britain around 1800 BC with migrants who used copper alloyed with tin to produce bronze. Suddenly there was a practical and decorative alternative to stone and wood – alternative and superior in its many qualities. The ores of copper and tin were present across the country, and mining developed. Smelting and casting could be applied to other metalliferous ores, and precious metals found their way to Dorset in the course of trade.

Round barrows, the burial-mounds of the Bronze Age, dominate the skyline in parts of West Dorset. For treasure-hunters and archaeologists they have been a rich source of material, because often they were the tombs of important people, who wanted to take their most prized possessions with them into the after-life. Weapons, tools and personal adornments throw light on the lives of such people. Sometimes a great hoard of material is found, as shown in the illustration, throwing up further mysteries.

The barrows beg many questions: were they only on hills, or were there many in valleys since ploughed-out by many generations of farmers? Why were there so many different designs, with ditches and banks around or at a distance? Why did subsequent settlers in later millennia, such as the early Saxons, open the barrows to bury their dead?

Remains of Bronze Age Barrows.

A Gold Lozenge
Dorset County Museum

IF TOOLS AND weapons were of more practical use to the people of Bronze Age Dorset, their culture encompassed some remarkable objects of fine art.

Foremost among the survivals of that fine art must surely be a gold lozenge found at Martinstown near Dorchester in 1882. It is a small metal sheet about six inches long, but it is made of high quality gold and is incised with a geometric pattern based on the mathematics of ten. To see it is to marvel at the extraordinary advance of humanity in a comparatively short time. The gold lozenge with its fine and careful designs has its fellow in a similar one found in Wiltshire. It is dated to a period towards the end of the second millennium BC.

It was found in a burial mound known as Clandon Barrow. No longer were people buried in communal graves. Bronze Age culture demanded separate interment with personal possessions. Clandon Barrow contained a decorated macehead, an amber cup and a bronze dagger, as well as the lozenge.

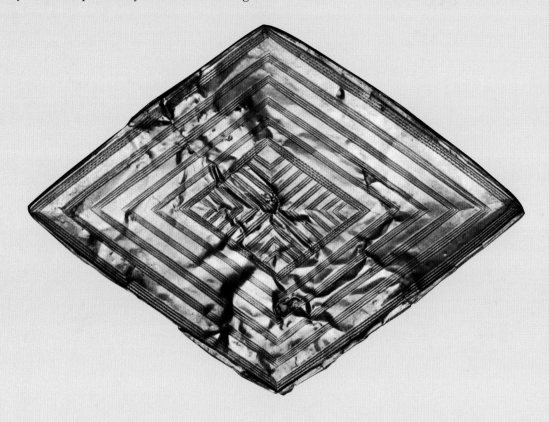

- 7 -
Iron Age Currency Bars
Dorset County Museum

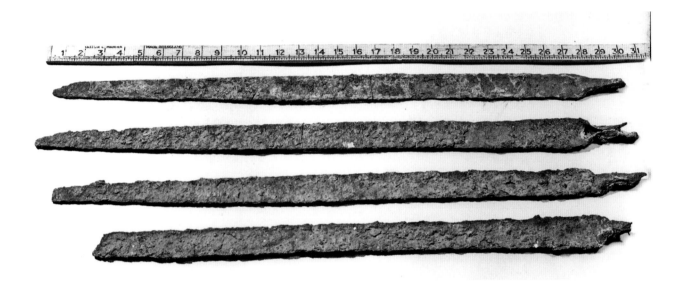

THE OLD SCHOOLBOY joke as an answer to the question 'How did they discover iron?' – 'They smelt it' – actually represents yet another amazing technological feat of the Ancient World. Like most other ideas the process came to Britain from the Continent, and it is extraordinary that someone somewhere had learned to put a lump of earth containing the element iron into a pit or oven with baked wood known as charcoal, lit it, closed it up and came back days later to find a bloom of iron.

The shapeless lump had then to be heated in a fire and hammered to remove the carbon, until it was almost pure iron. It was then malleable and could be worked into a required form. Iron was superior to bronze in that it was easier to obtain, cheaper, and

stronger in certain respects – though it would go rusty. To make an iron tool or weapon both strong and rigid it had to contain just the right amount of carbon – too much and the metal would break; too little and it would bend. The aim was to create steel, and that was highly skilled.

The Iron Age is considered to have reached Britain about 700BC. Thereafter the development of agriculture, the metal, textile and pottery industries grew apace and with them came trade. Some means of exchange had to be devised, and the iron currency bar filled the bill. It was valuable in itself, but it could be rated against other products. It is a curiosity that currency bars with their pinched handles were so much like swords.

An Iron Age Logboat
Poole Museum

BEAUTIFULLY DISPLAYED in Poole Museum is a large fragment of ancient and rotted timber. It has pride of place in the vestibule of this modern museum, and with very good reason.

The remnant is one of the earliest-surviving logboats, and is estimated by carbon-dating to have been constructed about 300 BC. Discovered during harbour-dredging in 1964, the hollowed-out trunk of a large oak tree is about 10 metres (33 feet) long, and might have carried up to 18 passengers though this is hard to imagine! A slightly larger dugout boat was found in Yorkshire in 1984, but the Poole boat remains a phenomenal artefact.

Although none was found, it is assumed that it would have been propelled with leaf-shaped paddles known elsewhere. Perhaps it was used to carry goods and people to the known trading settlement on Green Island. One thing is certain: the boat could never have left the comparatively calm waters of Poole Harbour, because it would have been extremely unstable and would have capsized in any kind of sea.

Ancient boats and ships brought up to the light are among the world's most exciting objects, but they are also among the most difficult to preserve. Left to the air, the logboat would have disintegrated rapidly. Left in water for thirty years and then soaked in a sugar-syrup solution for another five – the Poole Logboat is saved for us to admire and marvel.

WHAT DID IRON AGE Dorset people look like?

We don't know, because only the tiniest fragments of their clothing have been found in their graves, the rest having rotted away. We do know that they made woollen cloth in considerable quantities together with linen produced from flax, and that for heavy duty they had leather.

The evidence for clothmaking is found in many Iron Age sites. Foremost are loom weights, weaving combs and spindle whorls.

Sheep had been kept by many communities since the late Stone Age, and the wool had gradually become whiter. As metal shears became available, so shearing was easier, and the wool could be graded for fineness. Wound on to a stick later known as a distaff, a yarn was produced by twisting and pulling. The spindle whorl attached to the end of the yarn could preserve the tension. A simple wooden upright loom was strung with vertical threads to create a warp, and then the stone or baked-clay loom weights were attached to the threads to hold them in place. Weaving followed, and bone weaving combs were used to push the weft threads up into close fit.

All this could be done in a round thatched house, but the weaving would have been done mainly outside in order to have light. After weaving, the cloth was washed to shrink it and matt the fibres. Sometimes it was used immediately to make coarse clothing, but 'finishing' or shearing the loose hairs could follow, to produce a smooth surface. Dyeing could be done at any stage, using vegetable colours. Trousers, skirts, shawls and cloaks are known to have been made, and trade in the valuable manufactures helped the prosperity of the Durotriges and other British tribes in the years before the Romans came.

- 10 -
An Iron Age Ploughshare Tip
Dorset County Museum

A SMALL PIECE OF wrought iron found at a site in Gussage All Saints represents the lives of most people living in Iron Age Dorset. Farming was the dominant theme because food, clothing and even shelter depended on it. The technology of living had developed far enough for agriculture to have found the pattern which was to sustain society for two millennia.

This small iron blade slotted on to a shaft, which was the business end of an ard. An ard was a primitive plough pulled by oxen or by men, and it scored a shallow furrow through the ground. Without a mouldboard, the sod could not be turned, and to produce even a moderate breaking of the earth for sowing the ard would have to be dragged across again at rightangles to the first cut. This tended to create small square fields, whose shapes can be seen on hillsides to this day.

A range of crops was grown, including wheat, barley, rye and oats. The harvest (tiny compared with today) was stored in pits or raised granaries. The corn was ground in quern stones, and the dough baked in clay-domed ovens. Grain was also fermented to make beer. Animal husbandry was very important, and there is plenty of evidence for cattle, sheep and pigs – the latter being domesticated wild boar. Meat and fish could be dried and smoked for preserving, though salt could only be had through trade. The importance of timber cannot be overstressed, and woodland management with coppicing was practised.

Iron Age field patterns.

IN THE CENTURIES BC wine and fish sauce were shipped around the Mediterranean in increasing quantities, using pottery containers known as 'amphorae'. Their pointed bottoms would have meant that they had to be placed upright in a bed of sand in the hold of a ship. The many fragments of amphorae found at Hengistbury Head at Christchurch indicate that here was a trading port through which the better-off denizens of Iron Age Britain might obtain some of their little luxuries. No complete amphora has been found, and the illustration is of a replica based on the material found.

Archaeology suggests that Hengistbury was a centre for both industry and trade. The plentiful supply locally of ironstones (more recently known as 'doggers') was the basis for a strong metal-working industry which included both silver and bronze as well as iron. Other industrial activity is shown in the evidence for the production of leather and hides. These manufactures were convenient return-cargoes in the flat-bottomed boats which would have found their precarious way across the Channel or along the coast to other settlements. The increasing sophistication of commerce is clear in the large numbers of coins, Celtic and Roman, that have been discovered.

Recent investigations suggest that there was another service available at Hengistbury for the intrepid mariners. Since their ships or boats were not very sea-worthy, an aid to stability would be ballast. The dry animal hides exported were much lighter than the heavy wine-pottery imported. Gravel could be easily quarried along the shore, and it formed an admirable base for lowering the centre of gravity in these high-sided vessels. Signs of 'quarry hollows' along the shoreline indicate that as the boats grounded the unloading and re-loading could be easily achieved. The *'saburrarii'* or shovellers then came into their own!

- 12 and 13 -
A Mirror and a Sword from the Iron Age
Dorset County Museum

WE CAN OPEN A small window into the lives of upper-class Britons in the late Iron Age by examining what they took to their graves. It so happens that two Durotrigian graves not many miles apart and dated to roughly the early first century AD have yielded objects which can help us to imagine the people who placed value on them.

The bronze mirror found at Portesham is sufficiently rare for us to say that the lady must have been very proud of it and of the jewellery found with it. Some Roman trinkets were there also: either these had been obtained in cross-Channel trade with Gaul, or the burial post-dates the Roman Conquest in AD 43.

The mirror is an artefact made with considerable skill and artistry. The back is decorated with geometric designs and flowing curves. The front has long since lost its polished surface which once would have reflected the face of this British noblewoman. By our standards, her life would have been hard and uncomfortable in a smoky hut, but then she would have had servants and the respect of those over whom her husband held sway.

The Durotrigian population was small and spread over many little settlements. The Romans did not disarm or massacre those whom they had defeated. They demanded obedience and taxes, and the 'Whitcombe Warrior' was buried with his long slashing sword. He also had his spear, perhaps for hunting, and some domestic tools such as a hammer and a file. The sword is particularly fine, and demonstrates that here was a man of means. It has always been the nature of the upper classes that they will socialise with their peers, and it is certainly possible that the Portesham Lady and the Whitcombe Warrior could have known each other in life. Today their most precious possessions are exhibited next to each other.

- 14 -
An Arrow in the Back...
Dorset County Museum

ONE OF THE best-known exhibits in Dorset County Museum is the skeleton of a young man with the head of a Roman ballista bolt lodged in his spine. The ballista was a form of Roman artillery, a mechanical crossbow which fired metal-pointed arrows.

The grave was found in the 1930s by Sir Mortimer Wheeler who was conducting his famous 'dig' at Maiden Castle. It was assumed

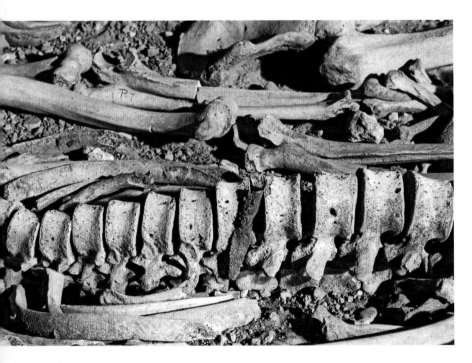

that here was a victim of the assault by the II Augusta Roman legion on the great hilltop fort, which had reached the flowering of a system of earthen ramparts and ditches developed over many centuries. Doubt has been cast on this reasonable assumption, because the cemetery excavated was found on re-examination to contain burials of differing dates and with causes of death unrelated to battle. And where are all the other casualties?

Maiden Castle is the largest example of hillforts developed by the Durotriges across Dorset. Its final phase of magnificent defences were no doubt intended to provide protection against the attacks of other British tribes, and the evidence of round huts and refuse pits suggests that in dangerous times a large township existed there. However, it may have been unoccupied at the time of the Roman invasion in 43 AD, and could have been surrendered after little more than a skirmish. This contrasts with the situation at Hod Hill near Blandford, where in a rather smaller fort there was considerable violence.

Prominent in both forts was the supply of slingshots, suitably-sized pebbles from Chesil Beach. Safe behind wooden palisades along the high ramparts, the defenders could rain down a hail of stones on the attackers struggling up the steep slopes. This may have happened at Hod: excavation of a round hut revealed that there was a shelf just inside the door where ready ammunition was stored.

Maiden Castle was abandoned, and remains as an open space to this day.

Maiden Castle.

ALL ROADS LEAD to Rome…in the old saying, but of course in the Roman Empire it was true. The imperial roads were intended to make rule from the centre more effective, with orders going out and taxes coming back, and legions marching to wherever there was trouble.

The enduring legacy of Roman roads was a pattern of communication which survives to this day, with modern roads often following Roman routes.

Five main roads can be recognised in Dorset, with a significant junction at Badbury Rings. The first runs from Hamworthy (a port) via Badbury to Old Sarum and thence eventually to London. From Badbury another road leads to Dorchester and then to Weymouth (the exact site of the port is not known). The third took the Roman traffic west from Dorchester and on to Exeter, and the fourth left Dorchester on a north-westerly route to Ilchester. The last of these main arteries was the road from Badbury in the direction of Bath. In spite of its strategic position as a junction, Badbury did not develop as a town and retained its prehistoric rings.

The Romans placed milestones on important roads, for two purposes: first to tell travellers where they were, and secondly to register the name and titles of the current emperor. It seems likely that the latter was regarded as the more important function.

A milestone found just to the east of Dorchester records a dedication as follows:

IMP POSTU MO AUG G

The Emperor Postumus Augustus

This makes it likely that it was set up between AD 260 and 269, when Postumus had rebelled against Rome and set up his own Empire in Gaul, Spain, and Britain. Unfortunately only the upper portion of the milestone survives, so there is no indication of how far it was to Dorchester. Since there is no absolute certainty that Dorchester was called Durnovaria at this time, a town name would have been helpful to us!

- 16 and 17 -
Two Roman Tombstones
Dorset County Museum and St George's Church Fordington

IN CHURCHYARDS ALL over Dorset are tombstones incised with details of the deceased. Most, even some of those from the 17th century, are legible. We have only two surviving from the Roman period, and those far from complete. There must have been many more, but the stone was far too valuable in its cut and ready state for succeeding and unheeding generations to ignore – and so was re-used in building.

One such was found in the 1980s at Wool. It is about a quarter of its original size, so perhaps the other three quarters are waiting to be found! It is the top right-hand quarter, and is incised with lettering of the last parts of words, leaving opportunity for speculation as to the full inscription. '-UNDUS' is probably part of a name, perhaps 'SECUNDUS' or 'VERECUNDUS' – which means 'bashful'! The bottom line is '-RALIS' which could be 'LIBERALIS' – 'gracious' or 'freeborn'.

Academic speculation suggests the stone could have commemorated two children, or possibly a Dorchester (Durnovaria) magistrate. Here is room for imagination!

The second tombstone is certainly of someone of high rank, and it survived as part of the material used in the porch of St George's church at Fordington. There is a replica in Dorset County Museum.

The tombstone is inscribed:

CARINO
CIVI-ROM
ANN-L
RUFINUS-ET
CARINA-ET
AVITA-FILI-EIUS
ET-ROMANA-UXOR

Carinus, Roman citizen, aged 50 years. His children, Rufinus, Carina, and Avita, with his wife Romana, [set up this memorial].

This stone dates from the early part of the Roman occupation and clearly Carinus was a man of importance, whose Roman citizenship meant he was not just one of the natives. Once again, imagination must come into play – was he a government official? Or was he a merchant involved in trade with this new market or source of supply? Since his family were with him, he was unlikely to have been just a casual visitor. We'll never know.

A "Roman" Fountainhead
Princes Street, Dorchester

A SUPPLY OF clean piped water may be called the first element of civilisation. Archaeology suggests that soon after the Roman army came to the Dorchester area in the mid first-century AD they established a fort, built an aqueduct to provide clean water for the military, and then diverted the final stage to reach the growing civilian settlement which became Durnovaria.

And you can still see considerable lengths of the aqueduct today! On the road from Loder's Garage towards Yeovil look left (if you're not driving) and the terrace can be seen clearly. Turn left at the roundabout and again the aqueduct appears – this time on both sides of the road because it follows the contour, and near the top of the hill the road crosses its course.

The watercourse itself was about a foot deep and nearly three feet wide.. To achieve a flow of about 13 gallons a second the route of the aqueduct had to follow closely the contours, and therefore winds its way round the hills from Frampton to Dorchester for about nine miles to cover a straight line of less than five.

The water probably arrived somewhere near the Top o' Town roundabout and was distributed to fort, houses and public baths by wooden water mains joined with iron collars. A public fountain would have been provided for general use, and today a small reconstruction in Princes Street commemorates the most likely site.

- 19 -
A Roman Force Pump
Priest's House Museum, Wimborne

EXAMPLES OF ROMAN water technology turn up all over the old Roman Empire. One such was found at Tarrant Hinton in the courtyard well of the Roman villa. It is a wooden block with twin cylinders and metal working parts – a Roman force pump.

It worked by human operation of a system of rods and levers (which have not survived). Water would have been drawn to the surface and stored in a tank, and thence piped as required.

How clean were the Romans? In 1977 part of a huge public bath complex was excavated, just south of Agriculture House near Waitrose in Dorchester. The dig turned up an extensive system of different kinds of bathroom, recreation rooms and reception rooms.

Hypocaust underfloor heating was evident in several areas, and the sauna bath was conveniently next to the cold plunge. Massages with oils would have been available, with food and drink to follow. Romans and romanised Britons could indulge themselves in the luxuries offered, attended by slaves: but this was an upper-class activity determined by both wealth and rank. One can imagine

the family who lived in the excavated Town House making good use of the facilities, but not the craftsmen who laid the tessellated pavements – though their washing needs might have been greater.

After the excavation the baths area was all filled in again, and a car park covers the site. The investigation showed that the buildings were in use for several centuries, and redevelopment (like today) was not unusual. The Roman baths used a great deal of water, and for a time the supply from the aqueduct must have been good. But the archaeology shows that the aqueduct went out of use only 100 years after it was built – so what did the Romans do for water then? Like many other interesting puzzles from the past, that question remains to be answered. Certainly there were wells, and probably other force pumps, though these have yet to be found. Can we imagine a chain of slaves passing buckets all the way up the hill from the Frome? Perhaps the buildings were simply used for other purposes, and the citizens of Durnovaria went dirty.

The Marks and Spencers Hoard
Dorset County Museum

IMAGINE THE FEELINGS of Mr McIntyre, the workman helping to clear the site at 48 South Street Dorchester, in preparation for the new Marks and Spencers store in the year 1936. As his pick bit into the earth, suddenly there were Roman coins – not just one or two (exciting enough) but hundreds, and then thousands.

Somebody in 3rd century Roman Dorchester put these coins in a large bronze bowl and in a bronze jug, and then buried them in the garden. Amazingly, there were 22,000 silver coins altogether, and they were almost all of the same denomination known as *antoniniani*: each about two days' pay for a Roman labourer.

Why did this citizen of Dorchester hide his loose change in the garden? Of course we can only speculate. The mystery deepens – many of the coins were mint-fresh, and had never been in circulation. Each coin had the head of the current Emperor on one side, and usually a soldier on a horse on the other.

Many Emperors are represented in the Dorchester hoard, but of the total 22,000 coins, nearly 9000 are of the Emperor Gordian III, and a further 5000 of Philip I. The whole range runs through the first half of the 3rd century, and the latest is dated to the year 257. The silver content varies, but a great debasement was yet to come – indeed it began in 258. One possible explanation of the buried hoard is that a businessman had been building up his capital, and as the new poor-quality coins began to come in decided to "bank" his good money in the only safe place he knew.

So why didn't he come back and retrieve his treasure? This is the mystery confronting the discoverers of all such hidden wealth. Perhaps he took his secret to the grave – death struck before he had a chance to tell anyone. Perhaps he secretly gloated every night about his secret store, and didn't wake up one morning. Perhaps robbers heard a rumour about his wealth and murdered him without finding it. Perhaps he was arrested for overcharging and sent to the galleys as a slave. Perhaps it wasn't a he but a she…what sort of business did she carry on in South Street?

- 21 -
Two Silver Spoons
Dorset County Museum

IN A ROMAN TOWN like Dorchester there would have been religious observance. There must have been temples, dedicated to the pantheon of gods which were at the centre of the official and compulsory forms of worship. So far, archaeology has found no sign of a temple.

However there is evidence of Christianity in 4th century Durnovaria. On a site near the centre of the town two silver spoons were found with Christian symbols engraved: a fish, and the words *'Augustine vivas'*. The spoons were buried with fifty silver coins – perhaps the treasure of a Dorchester church. In the cemetery at Poundbury about 1000 burials were laid out in Christian fashion (facing east and with hands crossed) and with occasional Chi-Rho decoration

Two Roman villas in the countryside have revealed even stronger Christian connections. At Frampton, among a wide variety of figures from classical mythology, a pavement depicted a roundel with the Chi-Rho symbol – the first two letters of Christ's name in Greek. More famously, and displayed on the wall in the British Museum, is the central panel of a pavement discovered at Hinton St Mary. It is a roundel showing the head and shoulders of a man (presumably Christ) in front of the Chi-Rho.

It seems likely that during the last century of the Roman occupation, religious activity was very mixed. After a period in which Christianity had been the official religion of the Empire under Constantine, the old gods (including Emperor-worship) made a come-back in the mid-4th century under the Emperor Julian. On Maiden Castle a temple and priest's house excavated by Sir Mortimer Wheeler has been attributed to this date. Probably the Celtic pre-Roman cults of the spirits of stream and forest had never entirely disappeared and surfaced again in the countryside. There is virtually no evidence as to the religious practices of the Britons in Dorset after the Romans left and before the newly-evangelised Saxons arrived 150 years later.

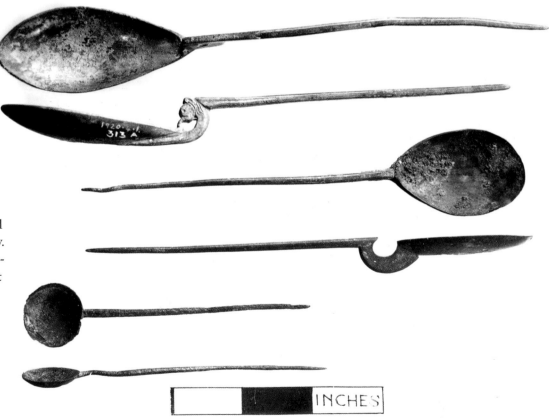

- 22 and 23 -
A Roman Table-Leg and a Mosaic Floor
Dorset County Museum and the Roman Town House

THERE IS A ROMAN house in the north-west corner of the town of Dorchester, just inside the town wall. The site was excavated by the famous archaeologist Sir Mortimer Wheeler in 1936, and the walls that he found have been preserved so that we can easily see the ground plan.

The house is evidence that some people in Roman Dorchester were quite rich, since the cost of building in stone was high. The building is detached, has some tessellated floors and has part central heating – all signs of wealth. It is thought that the house was built about 300 AD, but it was extended about forty years later, and abandoned in the last part of the fourth century when Roman rule was beginning to break down. The occupants were probably Romanised Britons – Celtic people of the Durotrigian tribe, who were rich enough to live in the Roman way, and may have spoken a kind of Latin. Otherwise, an Italian corn merchant or a government official from Rome may have lived there.

There are two ranges or wings to the house. The west range has tessellated floors and a hypocaust (underfloor heating). The furnace outside the house would have been stoked with wood by a slave, the smoke and hot air circulating among the pillars of tiles supporting the floor and then finding its way up the box flues in the walls and out to the air.

The south range has a verandah, which was a covered way along the side of the house with one side open above waist level. Only one pillar survives. There is another heated room, a kitchen and a servants' room.

The tessellated floors which can be seen have pleasant designs,

and were probably made by a master-mosaicist, a craftsman working in the town. We know this because there are many similarities between these designs and others found in Dorchester and in Roman country houses (known as villas) in Dorset and Somerset: this craftsman may have had a book of designs which he showed to prospective customers. The special features would have been made up in his workshop, carried carefully by cart to the site, laid in the chosen spot and finished off by infilling with other tesserae. The most complete example is in one of the smaller rooms, and is a fine specimen.

The walls are made of pieces of flint, with layers of limestone to bond or hold them together. They were plastered inside and out to give a smooth surface. The plaster was brightly coloured – outside it was red. The house had only one storey, and it was roofed with slabs of limestone on heavy wooden rafters.

Whoever planned the house seems to have had some regard for proper cleaning. The floors of the rooms are all on slightly different levels, so that when a bucket was emptied over the floor of the highest, the water would find its way into the next, and so on through the house until it reached the sump or drain outside the door of the lowest room.

At least the slaves did not have to go down to the river for water since there was a deep well in the yard. It is even possible that water was piped from the great cistern or tank at the top o'town, which was fed by the aqueduct still to be seen running along the valley slopes to the north.

Later builders used the stone from Roman ruins all over

Dorchester, which is why only the lower walls remain in this house. One piece of Roman furniture did survive: the carved leg of a table made of shale (an oily stone found near Swanage near Kimmeridge). It is unique, since no other Roman furniture has been found in Britain.

The House was given an all-over roof in the 1990s, with transparent side panels for easier viewing. It is hoped to make the site more accessible and better-protected when funds permit.

The Roman town house.

An Early Saxon Shield-Boss
The Red House Museum, Christchurch

ROMAN AUTHORITY in Britain ended in the early 5th century AD. The Legions departed and the Britons were left to organise themselves and to deal with the incursions of Germanic invaders from the continent of Europe.

In Dorset a curtain comes down. Archaeological evidence for the lives of the inhabitants in the next few hundred years is extremely scarce. Dorchester seems to have fallen into ruins as the thinly-romanised Durotriges reverted to their traditional tribal government and economy.

The Saxons who had been raiding the eastern shores of Britain while the Romans were still here began their permanent settlements in the early 5th century, and gradually moved west. A substantial invasion took place in the area of what is now Southampton, and then moved north, but Dorset was left alone.

There is only very scattered evidence of early Saxon presence, and this includes a 6th century cemetery just outside what later became the town of Christchurch. The cemetery indicates a settlement – but it did not last long. Some of the graves had grave-goods, and this shield-boss lay alongside a spear. The rest of the shield has rotted away, but it represents the valuable and necessary equipment of a Saxon settler in a foreign and hostile land.

Meanwhile Dorset remained as a British enclave for possibly two hundred years. Perhaps it was well-defended – the contemporary chronicler Gildas says that the Saxons were defeated at Mons Badonicus, which some have identified as Badbury Rings. Eventually the Saxons seem to have found their way round the north of the Durotrigian territory, but the absorption into what became Wessex was very late, and may have been a mingling rather than conquest.

The Saxon Angel
St Michael's Church, Winterbourne Steepleton

CHRISTIAN ACTIVITY in early post-Roman Britain is well-attested by cemetery evidence such as that at Poundbury, just outside the Roman boundaries of Dorchester. A building there may even have been a church, though how long it survived is not clear. There is a strong possibility that among the Britons in Dorset not only the worship of Roman gods continued at the same time, but that the pre-Roman Celtic religion came to the surface once more.

The progressive conversion to Christianity from Rome of the heathen Saxons in the 7th century can only have touched the fringes of Dorset, but the appointment of Aldhelm as Bishop of Sherborne in 705 seems to have been vital in bringing the ancient British tribal territory of the Durotrigians into the fold.

Thereafter the establishment of 'minsters' across the diocese created 'mother' churches, staffed by communities of priests who would serve over a wide area. This practice led to many such towns and villages including 'Minster' in their names. Preaching-crosses visited by minster priests sometimes gave place to churches – wooden at first until expensive stone could be used. The latter development often had to wait for the better times of the Middle Ages, and hence very few Saxon church buildings survive. St Martin's at Wareham is the best example, though substantially altered and restored. The familiar pattern of parishes grouped round a mother church seems to have been mainly established by the 10th century.

Although so little Saxon architecture remains, a few items of church decoration have been re-used in subsequent building. Notable among these is the 'Saxon Angel' at Winterbourne Steepleton. He lies reclining on his side, in an impossibly-contorted position, and was probably one of a pair, or part of a large crucifixion scene. By the time he was created around the year 1000, the Christian Church had survived the onslaughts of heathen Vikings and Danes.

A Royal Grave in Sherborne
Sherborne Abbey

BY THE YEAR 800 AD, the Saxons were well established in Dorset, having finally penetrated Celtic defences, or possibly they had just intermingled. The consequences are apparent to this day in the place-names and in the names of natural features. Most villages have Saxon or Norman derivations, while rivers are Celtic.

Dorset was part of the kingdom of Wessex, and Wessex was one of several Anglo-Saxon kingdoms across England. In the 9th century Wessex was dominant, but the whole country faced a new wave of invading barbarians. The Norsemen – Vikings and Danes – started with coastal raiding, and the first attack on Wessex was recorded in South Dorset about 790 AD. By the middle of the next century the raids on both sides of the English Channel had developed into casual invasion.

The King of Wessex at this time was Ethelwulf, who as a very religious man went off to Rome to visit the Pope. On his way back he called on the King of the Franks before crossing the Channel, and married his host's daughter by way of cementing an alliance against the corsairing Danes. While he was away his two elder sons had been left to look after the kingdom, east and west respectively. Ethelwulf died soon after his return and the elder son Ethelbald succeeded, and married his widowed stepmother Judith.

The only contemporary description we have of Ethelbald says he was 'unbridled', 'wicked' and 'froward'. When he died he was buried in Sherborne, as was his brother Ethelbert who reigned for about five years and had a rather better press. Two more brothers, Ethelred and Alfred, continued the battle against the Danes. Ethelred died after a battle in 871. This left Alfred, and we all know about Alfred the Great.

Alfred benefited from a very good public relations officer – himself. His biographer Asser was his loyal servant and recorded faithfully what Alfred wanted recorded. He undoubtedly achieved a great deal, driving out the Danes, encouraging learning and the arts, and establishing law and order. Unlike his brothers he survived for a long reign of thirty years.

Meanwhile, in Sherborne Abbey there are two huge stone coffins, in one of which there are bones open to view. By ancient tradition they are the bones of Kings.

An Anglo-Saxon Charter of 965 AD
Dorset History Centre

THE OLDEST DOCUMENT in the Dorset County archives is a Charter listing rights granted to 'Wulfheard' by Edgar, King of England 944-975. The Charter is in Latin, but is clearly legible, and it records the donation of three virgates of land at Cheselbourne. A 'virgate' was about thirty acres, so this was not a tremendous estate, but eventually it passed into the hands of the Abbey at Abbotsbury and the document survived in the monastic records. When the monasteries were dissolved by Henry VIII a great deal of their land, with supportive charters, went to the gentry, and some of the records were maintained – as in this case. It is not possible to distinguish from the Charter the exact location of the land granted, though it seems likely to have been near Puddletown.

Who was Wulfheard, and what did he do to deserve this grant of land? We don't know, and this Anglo-Saxon landowner flits on and off the page of History. The grant made him free of all dues except the obligations for army-service, bridge- and fortress-building. Since this was the reign of peaceable King Edgar, Wulfheard may very well have had no call for his services – though perhaps his descendants were called-up to fight the Normans in 1066.

- 28 and 29 -
The Wareham Sword – and a Leaden Casket
Dorset County Museum and Shaftesbury Abbey Museum

SIX HUNDRED YEARS of Anglo-Saxon Dorset have left rather fewer objects for study than might be expected. It is perhaps significant that several Anglo-Saxon survivals represent violence. One important find occurred in 1927 at Wareham – a magnificent sword, dated to the 10th century because of the inlaid decoration on its guards. The name of the owner is incised on the horn handle grip, but cannot be deciphered.

The recent discovery of a huge grave on the line of the new road to Weymouth has sparked off much speculation. Fifty decapitated skeletons of young men whose DNA shows strong Scandinavian connections, dated roundly to the 10th century, make it likely that they were a captured Viking raiding party. The savagery of the period, together with the fear of the settled Anglo-Saxons in the face of the terrible and terrifying Norsemen, suggest a mass execution.

It was not a new situation. The first recorded Viking raid on Dorset is dated to 793. The Scandinavians were exploding as their population outstripped the economy. The Swedes went to Russia, the Danes and Norwegians crossed the North Sea and explored possibilities in France, Spain and in the Mediterranean. Some even crossed the Atlantic.

Large numbers settled in the north and east of England. The smaller Anglo-Saxon kingdoms resisted ineffectively, but the kingdom of Wessex led by Alfred the Great fought back. Gradually

the area known as the 'Danelaw' came under the sway of Wessex, leading to the first Kingdom of England. In the reign of King Edgar 959-975, there was relative peace.

But then…Edgar was succeeded by his young son. Edward's character is uncertain – doubts were expressed – but he did not have much time to show it. In 976 he held a Council of the Wessex nobility at Puddletown (yes, really). Two years later he was hunting in Purbeck and decided to call on his widowed step-mother and her son Ethelred at Corfe. As he arrived some of Ethelred's retainers stabbed Edward to death in the saddle. Since Ethelred was too young to have organised this, it seems probable that it was down to the ex-Queen Elfthryth, said to have been beautiful but wicked.

Ethelred the Unready had an unfortunate reign. His late brother became venerated as Saint Edward the Martyr, and his remains were translated to a popular shrine at the nunnery at Shaftesbury: miracles followed. The leaden casket shown in the Abbey Museum today is strongly held to be the receptacle of his bones. In due course Shaftesbury Abbey was bequeathed large estates by the faithful, and became the richest monastery in Dorset.

The Danes renewed their attacks, and Ethelred's attempts to buy them off with 'Danegeld' were unsuccessful. Early in the 11th century England became part of the Danish kingdom; a brief spell of independence under Edward the Confessor was ended after his death by the Norman Conquest in 1066. The Normans were originally Vikings who had settled in France. Indirectly the Norsemen had won in the end!

So – the massacre on the Ridgeway could have occurred at almost any time in the 10th or early 11th centuries. Since this was the latter part of the 'Dark Ages', no written record of the event

Shaftesbury Abbey.

survives. We can only imagine the circumstances. Perhaps several 'longships' pulled into the estuary of River Wey, found only a few fishermen's huts and marched inland burning and pillaging the villages and farms. The King's Reeve in Dorchester would have summoned the 'fyrd' (the local militia or 'Dad's Army'), and then appealed for help from the King. The Vikings were hard drinkers – before going into battle they would get roaring drunk on mead, going 'berserk' and unable to feel wounds – so it is possible the raiders were caught senseless and captured, with the inevitable consequences. We may never know.

Corfe Castle
Corfe in Purbeck

IF THERE WERE no other evidence to mark the Norman Conquest and the end of Anglo-Saxon England, then castles would be significant markers. The Normans came and saw and conquered, but king and barons were aware that they were in a minority, and that they must establish their power over a potentially hostile people.

Heavily defended strongholds were seen as effective in two ways: both as refuges in time of revolt, and perhaps even more important, as images of the immense and unassailable power of the conquerors. There were royal castles and there were baronial castles, and Dorset has fine examples of both. As befits the king himself, the royal castle of Corfe is both dramatic and impregnable.

Even in its ruined state, Corfe still has the capacity to astonish the traveller as he suddenly turns the corner to see the solid stone walls far above on the top of the hill.

Although there might well have been a Saxon wooden hall before, the oldest stone construction is the wall around the top of the hill, and this is likely to have been built by 1080. Domesday Book, which surveyed the greater part of England in 1086, mentions 48 castles, and one of them is Corfe in the Manor of Kingston – though it is listed as Wareham Castle.

The strategic advantages of Corfe, providing a centre for control of Purbeck and Poole harbour, were recognised by successive monarchs, and for the next two centuries the castle was developed and extended. The great stone keep, inner and outer baileys protected by curtain walls with massive towers, gatehouses, ditches and drawbridges, together created a stronghold which could not be breached with the implements that attackers could wield at the time. Even the advent of cannon and gunpowder made little difference. When the castle was besieged by the Roundheads in the Civil War in the 1640s, the little guns which could be hauled up on to the hills either side of the castle were not able to make much impression. In the end the castle fell, but only because of treachery. To prevent any future resistance to Parliament, Corfe Castle was 'slighted' in 1646, thus creating the picturesque ruin we have today.

The Tabernacle in Milton Abbey
Milton Abbas

THE TABERNACLE in Milton Abbey church is an extraordinary survival. It is a small hanging cupboard in which was kept the consecrated bread, or Host, for the service known as the Mass. It is unique in that it is made of wood – most tabernacles or pyx-shrines were of stone. It is beautifully carved in an elaborate Perpendicular style, and it is painted.

Milton Abbey had a long history of radical change, destruction and rebuilding, before it finally succumbed to dissolution by Henry VIII. The Abbey church survived to become the parish church for the village of Milton Abbas, only for the village to be removed by the 18th century Lord of the Manor to improve his view.

The monastery was established under the Benedictine Rule in 964 by the Saxon King Edgar. Its income came from rents paid by tenants of the extensive land holdings, and from the wool crop of the monastic sheep. By the thirteenth century wool was the biggest English export, mainly going to the cloth manufacturers of the Low Countries and of northern Italy.

A huge fire destroyed the Abbey church in 1309. Rebuilding dragged on for 200 years, and it was never finished. The main problem was money. Taxes had to be paid, and some of these were taxes paid to the Pope.

Italian merchants on business in England were entrusted to collect for the Pope. Sometimes the Abbot could not pay, and the Italian merchants offered loans on the security of future wool crops. Such loans could be raised for the re-building, and elaborate plans for an enormous church were drawn up.

Stage by stage the church progressed, beginning with the eastern end, but there were long pauses. Crises such as the Black Death, and heavy criticism of the monks' behaviour by the Bishop, did little to help. Precious possessions of the monastery such as plate and jewels were pawned. The main rebuilding took place under Abbot William Middleton at the end of the 15th century: the central tower was completed together with much of the vaulting of the chancel.

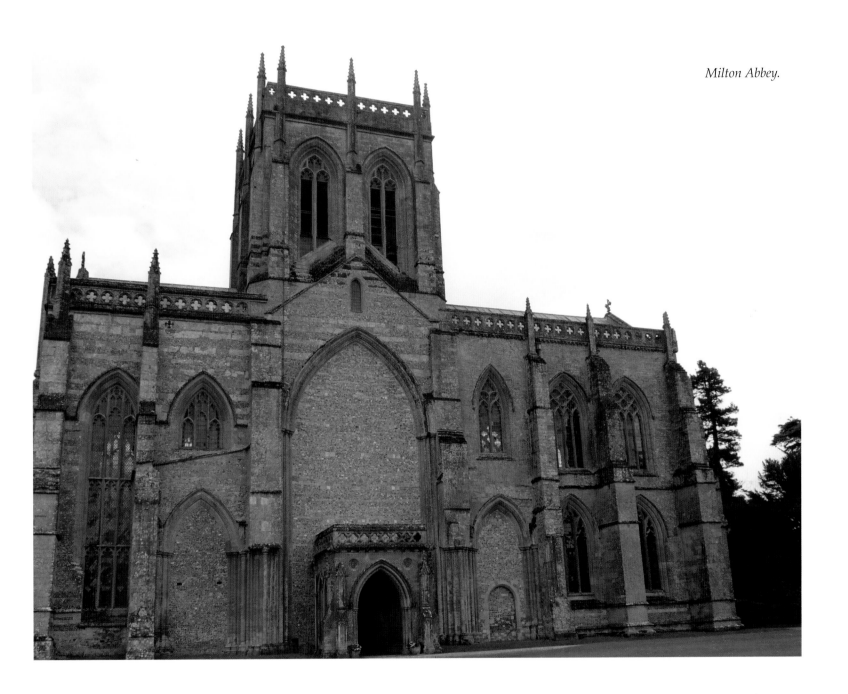

Milton Abbey.

But when Henry VIII's Commissioners came to call with the Deed of Surrender in 1539, the church was far from complete. The huge nave had not been started. Impressive as it is today, Milton Abbey church is only a fragment of what might have been.

A Mediaeval Decorated Floor Tile
Shaftesbury Abbey

EAST DORSET has a wealth of clay suitable for fine pottery. This resource was increasingly exploited from prehistoric times, but it was only in the later Middle Ages that the decorative potential of tiles for special flooring was realised. The technique of inlaying white clay allowed interesting designs to be devised.

Across the county mediaeval tiles survived, but mainly in fragments as old floors were replaced. Sometimes a single tile has to represent what was once a splendid pattern, as in this tile at Shaftesbury Abbey.

Sometimes tilers were itinerant, commissioned to undertake a particular job. A kiln would be built, but when the floor was complete the kiln would be demolished and the site buried. It is therefore not surprising that no mediaeval tile kiln has been found in Dorset. More permanent tileries existed in Hampshire, which produced what is known as the 'Wessex' pattern and many of these tiles were brought in to Dorset in the fifteenth century.

Tiled floors were mainly laid in the chancels of monastic churches, but some twenty-three parish churches in the county have been shown to have had them. A few manor-houses also had decorated tiles, but few have survived. Essentially tiles were a luxury item, and only richer clergy could afford them, as at Milton Abbey.

Gold Hill, Shaftesbury.

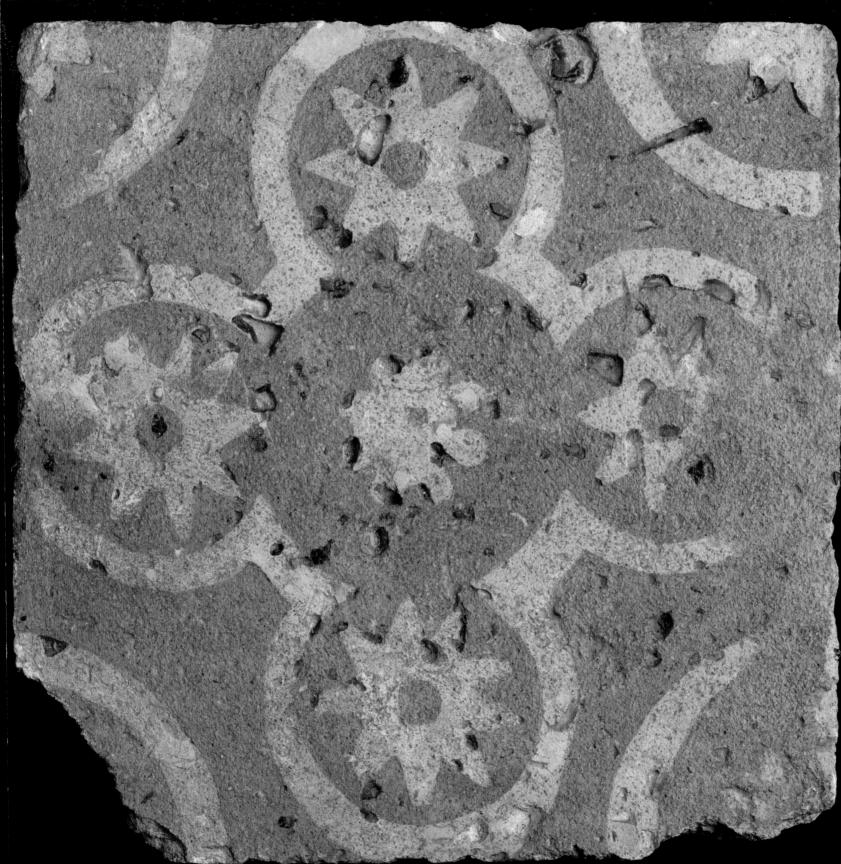

Radipole Rectors' List
St Ann's Church, Radipole, Weymouth

IN MANY COUNTRY churches there is a board showing the names of all the known Rectors and Vicars. Often this list begins in the 13th or 14th centuries, and certain significant dates can be recognised: changes of priest during the volatile period of the Reformation for example.

The plague known as the 'Black Death' struck England in 1348, and this is reflected in the high proportion of new parish priests appointed at this time. Clergy carrying out their duty of visiting the sick were particularly vulnerable.

The Black Death was a bubonic and pneumonic infection passed on by fleas from infected rats. A great wave of desperate illness spread from Asia across Europe, conveyed overseas by ship-borne rats. The shock to society was enormous – the evidence suggests that in the areas affected between a third and a half of the population died. In modern terms it might be compared with effects of nuclear war. People were helpless in the face of an enemy they could not see or understand, and against whom there appeared to be no defence.

The immediate effect was hardship. In a society totally dependent on successful agriculture, sudden removal of many of the workforce meant that crops could not be harvested or animals tended, and whole communities disintegrated with the survivors wandering in search of succour. Deserted village sites are evidence of the cataclysm to this day: see Object 36.

As the economy slowly recovered, profound social change took place. The bonds of feudal society were weakened, and serfdom gradually broke down as the peasants began to realise their rarity value. Lords needed tenants and labour, and after episodes like the Peasants' Revolt of 1381 were forced to adapt to new relationships over the next two centuries.

In Radipole church is the evidence illustrating the origin of these changes. The Rectors' List shows two new appointments in 1348, and it is known that the Black Death came to England first in a ship from France which docked in Melcombe Regis in that year.

Melcombe was a small town on one side of Weymouth harbour, and it was part of the parish of Radipole. The Rector of Radipole would have come down from the village to minister to this populous part of his parish, and so put himself in terrible danger – and so did his successor.

Melcombe Quay.

A Seal of the Borough of Poole
Dorset History Centre

Official matters of the Borough required authentication. Signatures might be forged, and only a proper Seal which was unique was good enough for proof of integrity. The Seal demonstrates the worthiness and vitality of the town in its depiction of a sailing ship – crucial to its future importance.

The ship has a single mast and a large square sail. The hull is clinker-built (ie with over-lapping planks, as in a traditional rowing-boat) and the nails are clearly shown. At either end there are wooden 'castles', which give defensible retreats in case of attack, and which can be used as vantage-points above potential enemies. The after-castle is much larger providing a 'quarter-deck', and perhaps also included accommodation.

Poole continued to prosper, had its first Mayor in 1371, the right to collect the King's custom duties in 1433, to have weekly markets and two annual fairs in 1453. In 1568 the town achieved the status of a County, separate from the County of Dorset, and with its own Sheriff – which it still has.

Ships meanwhile had developed into ocean-going multi-sailed vessels with great capacity, but that early seal is a sign of things to come.

THE PORT OF POOLE was a new town in the European boom period of the twelfth and thirteenth centuries. The silting-up of the channel up to the ancient settlement of Wareham had led to the beginnings of trade on the Poole peninsula, where there was deep water within an extensive harbour. Opportunities for business with markets across a newly-pacified Europe led to a community of prosperous merchants looking for control of their own affairs and freedom from the vagaries of a Lord of the Manor of Canford.

As always, money talked, and William Longespee felt able to grant their request for a Charter of rights in 1248, in return for 70 marks. The cash helped him on his way to defend the Holy Land in the Seventh Crusade, in which he was killed: the Borough of Poole now had its own Town Council and its own courts.

FOR A SMALL VILLAGE the church of Saint Candida and Holy Cross at Whitchurch Canonicorum is amazingly capacious and extravagantly built. That there was money to build so splendidly may well have been due to the fame of the shrine of Saint Wite. The income of the church went largely to the Canons of Salisbury and Wells, so the magnificence of the church must be due to their approval.

Local tradition says that Saint Wite was a Saxon woman who was murdered by marauding Danes when they landed at Charmouth in 831. No other information is available, though various stories have been advanced.

The shrine is built against the interior wall of the north transept, and is a simple stone box in the top part of which is a lead casket containing the bones of a woman thought to be about forty years old.

The practice of venerating Holy Relics – items which had a connection with a saint – had developed into something of an industry by the 13th century, which involved both tourism and commerce. Since medicine was still very primitive, it was inevitable that people should look for cure in the supernatural.

To touch or be near objects associated with a saint was understood to be the best means of communication. If seeking such relics brought hardship or expense, then this would prove piety and therefore deserve reward.

The fame of the shrine of Saint Wite as a place where healing might be found spread far. The pilgrims placed their diseased limbs, or small personal possessions, in the convenient oval holes at the base of the tomb. They also left their contributions in money. Saint Wite was not in the same league as St Thomas, some of whose followers have been preserved forever in the *Canterbury Tales*, but the money at least partly went to provide the great parish church.

The Reformers of the 16th century saw the pilgrimage industry as a corruption of the principles of the True Faith. Saint Wite remains today as the only shrine in a parish church to have survived the wholesale destruction of shrines at the Reformation.

- 36 -
A Deserted Village
Winterborne Farringdon

BETWEEN WINTERBORNE Came and Winterborne Herringston the ruins of a church stand out in the fields. They mark the site of a one-time settlement with farmhouses and a village street called Winterborne Farringdon. Earthworks still visible indicate the house-platforms, and the open-field strips show clearly.

It has to be said that the church gable-end is not entirely original, having been partially rebuilt with materials from other ruins. Nevertheless, there was a thriving community here in the 13th century, and a stone church was built by someone with money. What happened to destroy it?

There are deserted villages across the country, and the evidence usually shows two possible explanations, or a combination of both.

The first, and perhaps more dramatic, was the Black Death. The plague is known to have arrived in England for the first time in Weymouth in 1348, and the infection spread rapidly through Dorset and then beyond. Mortality was severe: estimates vary but overall it seems likely that between a third and a half of the population of the whole country died. Since some areas escaped altogether, this means even greater death-rates in affected neighbourhoods.

Such cataclysmic depopulation would have rendered the remaining community helpless. There was not enough labour to carry on harvesting, ploughing, sowing, or tending the animals, and the survivors might well have fled to the towns or to uninfected areas. In time the humble cottages would have rotted away, and even the church walls tumbled.

The second possibility is that the village was conquered by sheep. Even if the demand for food-production had diminished because of the Black Death, there was an increasing market for wool and for woollen cloth in Europe and the Middle East. The price of wool rose, and landowners saw the advantage of raising large numbers of sheep instead of renting their land to tenants. Evictions became more frequent, and homeless families became vagrants, with consequent social problems. 'Shepe eateth menne', as the situation was described in the early 16th century.

So what happened at Farringdon? One, or the other, or both? Or something else entirely? Take your pick. But it is a very picturesque ruin.

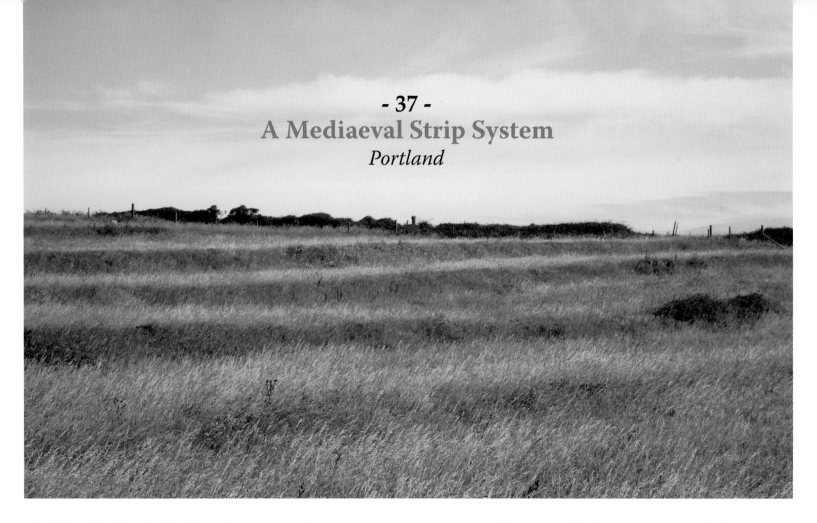

- 37 -
A Mediaeval Strip System
Portland

COMMUNAL FARMING with land held in small strips was the traditional and very widespread pattern in mediaeval England. Its origin may have been Saxon, but it was reinforced by the Normans and developed as part of the power structure later known as feudalism.

A lord ruled over an area known as a 'manor', within which a community operated a system in which farmers owed allegiance, service and dues to the lord. The system was controlled by age-old custom, which anybody defied at their peril. Attempts to improve meant change, which was suspect and resisted.

Change is inevitable, but in feudal England it was very gradual. From the 15th century through to the 20th, the manorial system slowly broke down, as demographic, commercial and political pressures broke through the cracks. The last legal vestiges were declared extinct in 1925, though such things as 'common' land, and empty titles of 'lord of the manor', still persist.

The open fields were divided into strips, and the common pastures, meadows and woodland, were gradually parcelled out, by agreement or Act of Parliament, into enclosed fields. Today only two examples of strip farming exist in the whole of England. One is at Laxton in Nottinghamshire; the other is in Dorset, on the Isle and Royal Manor of Portland.

At one time much of Portland was farmed in strips, but this was slowly whittled down and the last few to survive are carefully preserved for posterity to see, as the Middle Ages live on. Traditionally, a strip was the area that a plough drawn by oxen could plough in one day – an acre. Its length was established by the distance at which the team had to draw breath and turn round – a furrowlong or furlong. Balks of unploughed earth were left between strips, though sometimes boundaries were marked by stones.

All this can be seen easily from the road to the Bill on Portland. A thousand years of agricultural history!

Bere Regis Church Roof
Bere Regis

TO LOOK UP IN Bere Regis church with the lights on is an amazing experience. The nave roof is supported by six huge tie-beam trusses, with arched braces. Projecting from the spandrils are carvings of the twelve apostles, almost life-size and brightly painted, and the central bosses are decorated with symbols associated with Cardinal Morton.

Who was Cardinal Morton?

John Morton was born at Stileham in the parish of Bere Regis, went to school with the monks of Cerne Abbey, and then studied at Oxford before being ordained as a priest. He became Bishop of Ely, and in the Wars of the Roses was associated with the Lancastrians and the party of King Henry VI. In effect he was a royal servant and member of the Lancastrian government, and with the victory of the Yorkists and the reign of Edward IV Morton was forced into exile.

Morton made his peace with Edward and came back, but his position was precarious and he plotted with Henry Tudor, Earl of Richmond, to overthrow Edward's successor Richard III. Initial failure led to his further exile, but he persuaded Richmond to promise to marry Edward's daughter Elizabeth. When Henry Tudor invaded and killed Richard III at Bosworth in 1485, Morton was in a powerful position in the new regime. The promised marriage took place and united the rival parties of Lancaster and York, effectively ending the long period of baronial war. Morton was advanced in the Church to become Archbishop of Canterbury and a Cardinal; in the government of England he became Henry VII's Chancellor – a position akin to Prime Minister, though the King had the ultimate power.

And all this is celebrated in the roof at Bere Regis. The local boy had made good, and Morton reputedly paid for this magnificent adornment to the church of his boyhood.

He was certainly rich enough, though his financial abilities are celebrated in the story of 'Morton's Fork'. The royal income was not enough for the King of England to cut a significant figure in the European power-struggle, and more had to be found. Cardinal Morton would tour the country in his splendour, condescending to lodge with the great barons. On being received lavishly, he would suggest that as the host was clearly well-off he could afford to make the King a generous loan. If the hospitality was rather mean, the argument was that the baron was obviously saving money, which would enable him to help out the King. Either way, the victim was on the prongs of the fork!

The Abbot's Porch
Cerne Abbas

A PICTURESQUE Tudor tower, framed by leafy garden trees; delicate oriel windows on two floors, an arch beneath with Gothic ribs – and a passage through to nowhere but more trees, bushes and shrubs: this is the Abbot's Porch at Cerne Abbas.

It is amazing. Uninformed visitors to the garden of Abbey House, catching the sunlight glinting on the windows, pause and even gasp. The Porch is a monument to five hundred years of piety on this spot, ended by the demands of secular politics. It was, of course, all about money.

Henry VIII needed cash to buy warships, guns and troops to fight a probable invasion from the Continent. He wanted a legitimate male heir to succeed him, and had divorced the barren Queen Katherine to marry Anne Boleyn. Consequently he had to face the wrath of Katherine's nephew the Emperor Charles V – who happened to be the richest and most powerful monarch in Europe. In order to make the divorce legal, Henry had had to deny the authority of the Pope, and most of Europe was firmly Roman Catholic. War with the Emperor or the King of France (or both) was only too likely.

The King was now Supreme Head of the Church in England, and therefore possessed the power to close all the monasteries and sell their lands. Someone – probably his Secretary Thomas Cromwell – put the idea in his mind.

The process began in 1535 with a "Visitation" in which the monasteries were inspected by Commissioners. The report contained exactly what was required: ie it confirmed all those long-circulating anecdotes about lazy and immoral monks, and it gave clear indications of the worth of their estates.

Cerne Abbey was roundly criticised. The monks played dice and cards, and kept women in the Abbey. The Abbot spent money on his mistress and children, and was guilty of "gross immorality". It is likely that the sins of the monks at Cerne were exaggerated. The monastic system had declined in the late Middle Ages from the high ideals and devotion evident in the 13th century, but the real problem lay in the huge wealth of the Church, and the consequent domination of secular matters over spiritual duties.

Following Cromwell's Visitation, the issue moved swiftly to the government's desired conclusion. The smaller monasteries were dissolved by Act of Parliament in 1536. Cerne was just above the line, but the bigger houses were encouraged to surrender themselves. Early in 1539 the King's Commissioners toured Dorset accepting the surrenders of the monks.

In fact most of the huge advance in the King's wealth from all the monasteries was rapidly dissipated as he had to sell the assets to make war on France. The new guns and cannonballs were expensive.

The Elizabeth Frink Statues
Dorchester

THE REFORMATION began in Germany as a protest against the perceived corruption of organised religion, but was soon linked with political and economic issues across Europe.

In England Henry VIII's break with the Pope was occasioned by his need for a legitimate male heir, and Protestantism followed. The attempted re-imposition of Catholicism by Queen Mary I was accompanied by the full force of the burning alive of heretics. More than 300 Protestants were martyred in a couple of years, leaving an indelible public fear and revulsion.

When the first Parliament of Elizabeth I restored the Church of England in 1559 there was no immediate Protestant revenge, although in the spirit of the times all the Queen's subjects were required to attend the Established Church. The situation changed dramatically in 1570. The Pope declared Queen Elizabeth a heretic, excommunicated her and announced that all Catholics were absolved from allegiance to her. In effect, this was encouraging English Catholics to rebel, to assist foreign invasion and to assassinate the Queen.

Parliament reacted as might be expected. Conformity to the Church of England was more strictly enforced, and Catholic priests as agents of a hostile power were forbidden to enter the country. The discovery of plots to overthrow the Queen and to put the Catholic Mary Queen of Scots on the English throne only served to make the authorities even more punitive, and both priests and those who aided them were accused of High Treason.

Devoutly Catholic young men were tempted to go abroad for training as priests, and then to return to England to minister secretly to Catholic cells. They did so knowing that if discovered they were likely to be tortured to reveal others and to be hung, drawn and quartered. When King Philip II of Spain sent his Armada to invade England in 1588 the national fear of Catholics was intensified, and so was the search for papist priests.

In 1585 Thomas Pilchard was captured and banished to France, but returned to London and was sent back to Dorset. He was executed in Dorchester at the gallows at the top of what is now Icen Way in March 1587. John Cornelius was captured in his hiding place in Chideock Castle and was brought back to Dorchester for trial and execution. Nearly fifty years later at the beginning of the Civil War the grisly scene was re-enacted for Hugh Green. The hysterical Dorchester crowd, driven to madness with fear of imminent attack by the forces of the King, played football with Green's decapitated head.

Thus it was these victims and others were recognised as martyrs by the Catholic Church. They are commemorated by the statues sculpted by Dame Elizabeth Frink at the end of South Walks in Dorchester, close to the spot where they suffered.

Icen Way, Dorchester.

John White's Pulpit
St Peter's Church, Dorchester

FOUR HUNDRED years ago Dorchester had its own municipal brewery at the bottom of South Street. The profits from the brewing of ale were considerable, and they went to fund a number of social services. Is this a pointer for reducing the Council Tax today?

In fact the early 17th century was outstanding in the provision of both public and private benefactions for the less advantaged of the town. John White, the puritan Rector of Dorchester inveighed against the display of private wealth as well as against the debauchery of both rich and poor. He urged the successful businessmen of the town to give large sums to the Rector's charities. These included the Hospital (not a medical centre, but an orphanage and industrial training establishment for poor children); Trinity School for young boys; and a Fuel House for the distribution of cheap firewood.

Inspired by the oratory in the pulpit, individual citizens bequeathed large sums to found Alms Houses: Napper's Mite, Chubb's, and Whetstone's.

Of these, Napper's Mite in South Street survives in much the same form today – though not with the same function. Sir Nathaniel Napier, who had land at Middlemarsh left money to set it up in 1615 for the care of ten deserving old men. Chubb's catered for women, Whetstone's for married couples.

The Puritan ethic was straightforward: hard work, moderate living, care of your neighbours. If God had chosen you to have absolute faith in Him, then you would go to Heaven. If you had not, then you must obey the injunctions of those who had, because it was their duty to show you the right way.

John White's Dorchester was a thorn in the side of the government. Puritans did not comply with the High Church regulation of King and Bishop. Government Ministers regarded the public provision for poor, sick and old outside the national Poor Law with suspicion. In these years before the Cavaliers and Roundheads were at each others' throats, Dorchester might well have deserved the title of 'The People's Republic of West Dorset'.

The Dorset Quarter Sessions Order Book 1625-1638
The Dorset History Centre

IN THE DORSET Record Office there is a substantial manuscript volume which contains the earliest record of the business of governing the County and dealing with matters of law and disorder.

As the name suggests, in the 17th century the Court met four times a year: at Blandford, Sherborne, Shaftesbury and Beaminster – and occasionally at Dorchester. The Sessions would last a few days. All the Justices of the Peace of the County were requested to attend, but in practice only a few of the most active did so. Justices were appointed by the Lord Chancellor, and were gentry – knights or esquires – and of course male. To be a JP was considered an honour but the duties were a matter of choice, and most magistrates were concerned with their immediate neighbourhood. In any case the borough towns had their own courts and magistrates.

There was no election for Chairman of the Court: he was just 'recognised', and at this time it was most often Sir Francis Ashley. Ashley was the Recorder of Dorchester, a distinguished lawyer and scion of a family which produced the Earls of Shaftesbury.

The formal doings are written in Latin, but the Orders made by the Court are in English. Much of the work was that which today is dealt with by the County Council and District Councils.

This included supervision of roads and bridges – Julian Bridge at Wimborne was always falling down. Housing matters encompassed the illegal building of cottages on common land. Wage rates and treatment of apprentices frequently came up.

Some of the more colourful cases reported concern bastardy. Unmarried mothers frequently required support, which under the Poor Law was supplied by the Parish Overseers of the Poor. They would attempt to recoup their expense from the putative fathers, who often denied paternity and were prosecuted.

Criminal work took up less time. More serious cases would be referred from Petty Sessions – magistrates sitting in their own locality – but the most serious would go to the Assizes and a Royal

Judge. Even so, penalties inflicted included fines, imprisonment, whipping, and the pillory. In only three instances was there a sentence of death, as almost all capital offences went to the Assizes.

A translation and summary of this volume is available in print from the Dorset Record Society.

- 43 -
The Cannonball in the Wall
Maiden Street, Weymouth

BY THE SPRING of 1645 the King was losing the Civil War with Parliament, which had at last reorganised its Army. In the previous three years the rival forces had swept backwards and forwards through Dorset, with the towns resisting and succumbing as the situation demanded. Broadly the towns sympathised with Parliament, and the landed gentry more with the King – though there were many exceptions on both sides.

Weymouth consisted of two towns: Weymouth and Melcombe Regis, either side of the harbour. On 9th February 1645 the Royalist Sir Lewis Dyve, with troops from Dorchester, supported an attack on Weymouth from the south by the Portland Castle garrison.

Landing from boats they smashed their way into the North fort on the Nothe and then captured the Chapel fort at Chapelhay above the bridge. The Parliamentary infantry (the 'Roundheads') retreated across the harbour into Melcombe and hastily threw up earthworks across the road from Dorchester.

Looking down on the town from Chapelhay the Royalists began a bombardment with the captured cannon, using red-hot shot. One of the balls remains embedded in the wall of the 16th century building in Maiden Street now used as a ladies' lavatory.

Lord Goring, based in Sherborne for the King, sent cavalry to protect a convoy of supplies for the Weymouth forts, and some Royalist infantry left the forts to help. Colonel Sydenham seized the opportunity for Parliament and led a storming force across the bridge and up the hill to Chapel fort, which was taken along with 160 Royalists.

Goring turned to another plan – a night attack across the Back Water. It was a secret plan, and Goring hoped that Royalist sympathisers in the town would help, using the codeword 'Crabchurch'. The secret was betrayed by a prisoner to Sydenham, and so he too prepared a secret plan. The Roundheads withdrew their troops from the area facing the inner harbour, and householders were ordered to leave their gates and doors open. Several hundred Royalists crossed the harbour in darkness with muffled oars and made their way unopposed to St Thomas Street. In a sudden blaze of musketfire they found themselves surrounded and rapidly overrun. It was said that two hundred and fifty were killed. Some escaped by boat and the remaining Royalists ran for Wyke Regis and then Dorchester.

Revenge on the Royalist townsmen followed and some were hanged as traitors. The fighting died out in 1646 and Charles I sought sanctuary in Scotland but was handed over to Parliament. The Army which had defeated him seized control of the Kingdom from Parliament in 1648, and executed the King in 1649. An English Republic had been achieved and lasted eleven years.

- 44, 45, 46 and 47 -
Fire over Dorset

Fire Hooks *(Bere Regis Church)* Fire Insurance Marks *(Wareham Museum)*
Fire Engine *(Gillingham)* Fire Helmet, Axe and Bucket *(Dorset County Museum)*

FIRE, WAR AND plague – all of these came to Dorset in the 17th century. Townspeople must have lived in constant fear of calamities which they could do little or nothing to avert. War and plague were comparatively rare, but fire could happen at any time. Domestic accident was often the cause, and careless cooking could mean a conflagration that destroyed many wooden houses and thatched roofs. In January 1629 a complaint was made to the Court of Quarter Sessions that Widow Gaye of Wimborne was brewing ale in her house using a wooden chimney, to the great danger of her neighbours. This was underlined when the house actually caught fire during the court sitting.

The biggest Dorchester fire ever was probably that of 6th August 1613, when the tallow chandler in High West Street briefly neglected his business. Dry weather and a lively breeze completed the job and within a few minutes the centre of Dorchester was ablaze.

There was no piped water and many wells were dry. People were hastily summoned back from the harvesting to form long bucket chains up the hill from the river. One great fear was for the gunpowder store in the Shire Hall, and the Bailiffs organised a party to wrap the barrels in wet sheets and roll them out to the fields. The wind came from the west, and the fire swept down the High Street and into the parish of All Saints. At the bottom of the hill stood the Prison, and the prisoners were let out to fight the flames – and they didn't run off! Only one person died, but 170 houses were burnt. Restoration took many years.

Firefighting was regarded as a local matter. A fire-engine owned and maintained by each parish consisted of a simple lever-operated pump on wheels, with a tank of water and a length of leather hose. More basic implements were poles with iron hooks, used for pulling burning thatch from roofs. The gear was usually kept in the church as at Bere Regis, and the churchwardens' accounts kept

Fire hooks, Bere Regis church.

Helmet axe and bucket, Dorset County Museum.

Fire marks, Wareham Museum.

65

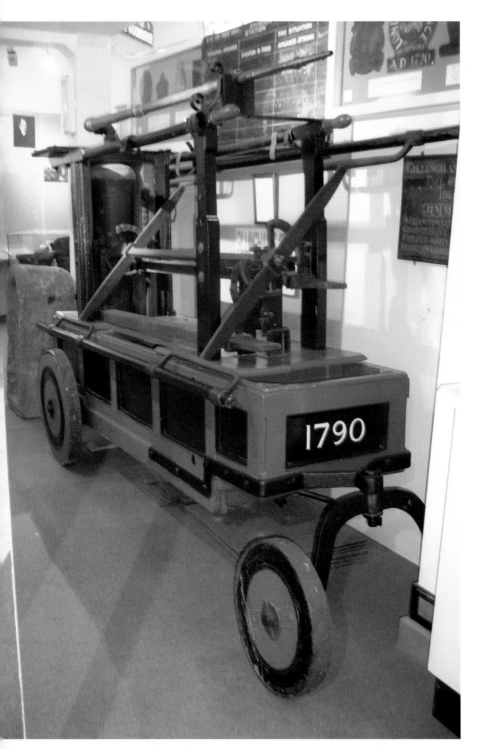

in the period show expenditure on frequent repairs to the 'injun'.

One of the results of the Great Fire of London was the development of Fire Insurance. Until then victims of fire could only petition for help from collections in church. Companies offering fire insurance spread from London to lesser towns across the country, and soon their distinguishing 'marks' began to appear prominently displayed on clients' houses. The plaques served to indicate to the private fire brigades which houses were due for their protection when fire broke out.

Blandford owes its beautiful town centre to a great fire in 1731. Following the anguish, horror and financial loss, the new buildings were constructed of safer brick and stone by the architects John and William Bastard.

By the 1890s several town Fire Brigades had advanced to the possession of uniforms and a large horse-drawn pump – still hand-operated and with a leather hose. The great improvement was the introduction of a steam-pump which increased the flow of water. The speed of action cannot have been very great: when the alarm was given, the firefighters had to be summoned, the fire under the boiler had to be lit, the horses had to be brought out and shackled to the appliance, and then there was a dash through the streets. You may guess the length of time before the fire engine arrived! At least a piped water supply gradually spreading through towns after 1860 must have helped.

Just before the outbreak of the First World War in 1914 many horse-drawn fire engines were replaced by motors, and the Fire Brigades began to look quite modern. Basic equipment remained however, including brass helmet, axe and bucket as displayed in Dorset County Museum.

The Second World War threw up entirely new problems and Fire Services were nationalised, being returned to local authorities in 1948. Dorchester has now acquired a magnificent Headquarters and Fire Station at Poundbury, with multi-purpose appliances devoted to Fire and Rescue. Townspeople must feel better protected than ever before!

Gillingham Fire Engine.

- 48 -
Abbotsbury Church Pulpit
Abbotsbury

IN THE THIRD YEAR of the English Civil War Parliament – the Roundheads – were beginning to prevail over the forces of the King – the Cavaliers.

In 1643 Dorchester had surrendered to the Royalists led by Lord Carnarvon and Sir Anthony Ashley Cooper, but a few months later Cooper dramatically changed sides, declared for Parliament and set about towns like Wareham, Poole and Weymouth. Usually he was welcome, but then attacks from Cavaliers in Sherborne and the West had to be resisted.

By November Cooper could find time to probe westwards and to help the Roundheads in Lyme Regis. On the way was a Royalist garrison occupying the Manor House in Abbotsbury.

Colonel James Strangways had fortified the mansion as well as the parish church just outside the gate. There was a strong wall and gatehouse, and the entrance could be protected by fire from the church. Strangways was invited to surrender, and refused, hanging a bloodstained flag from a window in a time-honoured gesture. The young Ashley Cooper, fiery and impetuous with supreme confidence at the age of 23, ordered the attack on the church. Major Edward Baynton led the assault on the porch, smashed his way in, and in a blaze of musket-fire subdued the thirteen defenders. To this day the holes made by the musket balls can be seen in the great Jacobean pulpit.

Still no surrender of the house, so the besiegers burnt the gatehouse and charged across the yard to the main door. This too was attacked with burning faggots, while the musketeers peppered the shuttered windows. Cooper had stationed a small cannon on the other side under the command of Colonel Sydenham, and its fire was concentrated on the upper storeys. Soon men were climbing scaling ladders, wrenching open the barred windows and hurling fireballs and grenades into the house. As the fires spread the defenders cried out for quarter, which the blood-lusted Cooper was disinclined to grant, but Sydenham's calmer view held sway and mercy was given.

At once the victorious Roundheads began to plunder. A hundred and thirty prisoners were hauled out, and as they went, grateful for their lives, they warned their captors to leave the house immediately because the fires would soon reach the gunpowder store in the cellar. Their advice was ignored, and the house exploded. Three dozen soldiers were killed.

Today the house that you see is a jumble of buildings with many interesting nooks and crannies: some survivals from the ruins left after the siege together with later additions and modifications. Standing between church and house today it is hard to imagine the carnage of that winter day.

Abbotsbury.

A 17th Century Warming Pan and a Stone Hot Water Bottle
Dorset County Museum

IMPROVEMENTS IN the standard of living, at least for the better-off, were noticed by contemporaries from Elizabethan times. A more comfortable night's rest could be achieved in a feather bed and with sheets rather than a straw-filled palliasse and rough woollen blanket. Without central heating even this better bedding could be cold on first acquaintance, particularly since in the 17th century it was not unusual to undress completely for sleep.

The answer lay in a warming pan. This was a round copper vessel with a hinged lid, into which hot coals or embers from the fire were placed. A long wooden handle made it possible for a maid to carry the pan to the bedroom, insert it beneath the covers and sweep it across the sheets. It could be left in the bed, but there was a risk of scorching or worse. If there were airholes in the lid, this allowed the embers to go on burning for longer, but increased the fire risk.

Famously, a baby was said to have been smuggled into the royal palace in a warming pan, to replace a still-born child when King James II urgently needed a male heir in 1688. True or not, the child did not help the King, as the thought of yet one more member of the Stuart family on the throne helped to provoke the rebellion which overthrew him. A group of aristocrats and gentry met at Charborough Park near Wimborne to plan what became known as 'The Glorious Revolution', which finally secured the supremacy of Parliament over the monarchy.

By the 19th century ceramic hot water bottles – safer and cheaper – were replacing warming pans, and their use became widespread before the advent of moulded rubber after 1900. During World War Two rubber was in short supply, because the Japanese had occupied Malaya. 'Stone' hot water bottles made a come-back, and when placed inside a large sock could maintain a reasonable temperature all night!

The Monmouth Bedhead
Lyme Regis Museum

JAMES DUKE of Monmouth was the illegitimate son of Charles II, and was something of an irresponsible ne'er-do-well who had fled to Holland. When he heard of his father's death he began a plot to take the throne from his uncle James II. The Earl of Argyll sailed to Scotland to raise a force there, and in June 1685 Monmouth landed at Lyme Regis with eighty men and called on disaffected westcountrymen to rally to his flag.

He established his base in the 'George' Inn. The Duke occupied

The head of the Bed in which the DUKE of MONMOUTH slept when he landed at LYME, JUNE 11th 1685.

the best bed in the house, and the carved wooden bedhead survives to be displayed in Lyme Regis Museum. The bedhead is a suitable memorial: it is lavish and elaborate in a pretentious baroque style.

The disaffection Monmouth expected was based on the lingering fear of Catholicism and the imposition of a despotic monarchy. James II was an avowed Roman Catholic and made no secret of his intention to control Parliament. In fact ordinary people had little knowledge of politics and the disaffection in Dorset and Somerset was largely economic – there was a slump in the cloth industry and unemployed cloth-workers naturally blamed the government.

Very few gentry supported Monmouth's cause.

Thus it was that the 8000 men who flocked to join Monmouth as he marched north towards Bristol were a ragged army with very few muskets and mainly equipped with agricultural tools such as hayforks and billhooks.

Initially Monmouth's march was triumphant, with civic welcomes at Taunton and Bridgwater, but soon there was news of a hastily-assembled Royal army on its way from London to quash the rebellion. When it arrived Monmouth was occupying Bridgwater, and when he tried to break out across Sedgemoor the King's troops quickly put paid to the rabble.

The Royal revenge began immediately: possibly two hundred rebels were hunted down and summarily killed. Monmouth was beheaded on Tower Hill, and James II ordered the Lord Chief Justice, Lord Jeffreys of Wem to carry out a special Assize to try the 1500 held in prisons in the West.

Jeffreys arrived in Dorchester on Saturday 5th September 1685 for the first of the big Sessions. Most of the defendants were sentenced to death, some to transportation to the West Indies. By the time he left on 10th September more than 300 had been sentenced. The Assizes continued in Exeter, Taunton, Bristol and Wells.

Three years later in the 'Glorious Revolution' another more successful invasion took place in Torbay, when William of Orange landed and overthrew James II – but this time it was supported by the squires and aristocracy and was reinforced with a Dutch army. It was the final establishment of rule by Parliament.

- 52 and 53 -
A 17th Century Chamber Pot and a Victorian Earth-Closet
Dorset County Museum

IN THE DORSET County Museum there are two objects which typify the age-old problem of disposing of human waste. The 17th century chamber-pot was used at a time when the contents might well have been thrown into the street with the old cry of "Guardy-loo!" – but it wasn't, because the pot was found in a refuse pit a couple of hundred years later, after the maid accidentally let go and declined to fish it out…

The second object is an earth-closet, invented by Henry Moule the Rector of Fordington in response to the horrors of cholera in Mill Street, Dorchester.

Mill Street today is a quiet corner of "Old" Dorchester, with the millstream running pleasantly down to the site of the mill, alongside restored cottages and retirement flats. It wasn't always so. For many years Mill Street was a centre of deprivation and depravity,

where revolting slums rarely saw a constable, and the denizens fought each other and the law to claw a living.

The trouble began long ago when an anomaly in authority left five acres of the Manor of Fordington around Mill Street as a "Liberty" of the estate of Bindon Abbey, separate from the Manor. Fordington became part of the Borough of Dorchester in 1835, but not Mill Street. The area was a refuge for the unemployed and homeless, especially families dispossessed in the farmers' zest for improving profits.

In the mid-nineteenth century the exploding population of Britain demanded more and more food. Farmers looked for productivity, and found the answer by dismissing their full-time labourers and employing gangs of workers at busy times like harvest. The gangmasters recruited their gangs in places like Mill Street. Employed for a few weeks, men and women would come home to spend their money on drink, and somehow survive until they were needed again. The filth and degradation of Mill Street offended the sober citizens of Dorchester, but it took a great health scare to even begin improvement.

In 1854 soldiers in Dorchester Barracks went off to the Crimean War. Millbank Prison in London was overcrowded, and cholera broke out. Dispersal seemed a good answer, and Dorchester Barracks lay at the end of the newly-built railway. Negotiations with the Town Council included assurances that only healthy prisoners, properly washed, would be sent. Unfortunately the blankets that came with them were not washed – but the washerwomen of Mill Street set to with a will and in anticipation of a good moneyspinner.

There was no piped water. The millstream was used for the laundry, as it was for drinking water. It was also the sewer, into which drained the privies and cesspits of the teeming hovels.

The result may be imagined. There was a cholera epidemic in Mill Street, and men, women and children died in large numbers. Public meetings were held in the Corn Exchange to explore ways in which the infection could be stopped from galloping up High East Street and engulfing the town.

Henry Moule, Rector of Fordington, acted heroically caring for the sick, and wrote a series of Open Letters to Albert the Prince Consort (published in *The Times*) urging that the Duchy of Cornwall should undertake slum clearance and reform. He also urged the virtues of the earth privy whose contents could be could be buried with sanitary care.

Dorchester did not succumb. Civic improvement in the late nineteenth century provided water, paved streets, sewers, hospital, lighting, a fire service and police. Gradually the iniquities of Mill Street diminished, but well into the 20th century its reputation stood.

- 54, 55 and 56 -
Mercy Weights, Stocks and Handstocks
Dorset County Museum and Corfe Castle Museum

DORCHESTER HAS HAD a prison since at least the 14th century. In the early 17th century it was rebuilt at the bottom of High East Street, on the north side near the River Frome and next to the White Hart. The prison was run by the county magistrates, who appointed the Governor and heard complaints and reports. Finance came from the rates which were collected in each parish across the county.

At that time prison was mainly a place to hold suspects until they were tried – punishments were usually physical or financial. Stocks were used in towns and villages across the county to punish drunkenness or minor disorder. The pillory was a much more

serious punishment since offenders were held standing to face public insults and missiles, which could result in injury. People who were fined were often sent to prison until they paid. Part of the building was designated as a House of Correction, in which vagrants, mothers of bastard children, hedge-breakers and others guilty of minor offences were kept and made to work.

Prison inmates had to pay for board and lodging, and would negotiate a fee with the Governor for a private room. Prisoners without funds were given a small allowance of bread daily, and lived communally in a large room. Dangerous people were shackled with 'fetters and gyves'. "Handstocks" were also employed for

this purpose as late as Victorian times. The Governor had the authority to inflict whippings as required.

Executions followed the twice-yearly Assizes presided over by a judge. The procession to the gallows at the top of Icen Way from the prison included the condemned standing in in a cart surrounded by guards and a crowd which might be hostile or sympathetic. Halfway up Icen Way stood an alehouse where traditionally the prisoner was given a last drink.

One of the unforeseen consequences of the American Revolution was that the former colonies were no longer available for the transportation of British criminals. Until a new destination was found in Australia, prisons suddenly became overcrowded, and Dorset magistrates became involved in the move to reform prisons as places for long-term incarceration. Accordingly a new site was

established on Castle Hill off North Square and in the 1790s a prison was built, planned on lines much approved by the reformer John Howard.

The new prison was set in a walled enclosure, and consisted of separate blocks for different kinds of prisoner, with individual cells and provision for useful activity. In the outside wall was a substantial gatehouse, which is the only part remaining today. The gatehouse served another purpose: the gallows was placed on top, and until public executions were abandoned in the 1860s onlookers could gather in the fields on the other side of the river to indulge their sadistic pleasure. A further refinement of the system was the introduction of "mercy weights". These metal bricks were attached to the legs of the condemned person and ensured a more rapid strangulation.

The Thornhill Obelisk
Near Stalbridge

AMONG SUCCESSFUL men the urge to leave a permanent and striking memorial of their lives can be very strong. Such memorials have taken many forms: some useful, some merely 'follies', and some demonstrating adherence to a Cause.

An example of the latter type is the Thornhill Obelisk. As befitting a gentleman steeped in Classical tradition it echoes a practice with roots in ancient Egypt and the Roman Empire. Reaching for the sky from the top of a hill, it is visible for miles, and it bears an inscription expressing joy for the Coronation of a Protestant monarch.

James Thornhill was born in Melcombe Regis in 1675 to a family which had once held the Thornhill estate near Stalbridge. Early signs of talent were recognised by apprenticeship for seven years to a decorative painter with London connections, and when James set up on his own his work was soon in demand. The burgeoning merchant classes of the late 17th century were building large houses in town and country, and the Baroque fashion for lavish classical and historical painted ceilings and walls was seized by Thornhill with enthusiasm.

The Protestant Succession after 1688, and a wave of Anglican patriotism together with the French Wars led Thornhill to royal patronage and a commission for the Painted Hall at Greenwich Naval Hospital, which took twenty years to complete. In 1718 King George I made him Court Painter, and knighted him in 1720. The boy from Weymouth had arrived!

In the same year the artist bought back the ancient family manor and began to live like a country gentleman. Through the goodwill of his friend George Bubb Doddington – a political fixer – he secured a parliamentary seat for the town of his birth. Local commissions came his way, including the decoration of the hall and stairs in the house in Sherborne occupied until recently by Lord Digby's School.

The accession and coronation of George II and Queen Caroline inspired James Thornhill to create a permanent monument to the Hanoverian Royal Family. The Obelisk on Spire Hill is a dramatic gesture recording the artist's loyalty and admiration. The classical tradition shows off his culture, and the fulsome terms of the Latin inscription perhaps indicated a hope for further royal patronage.

Thornhill died in 1734. The Obelisk survived a further century, and then it succumbed to a great storm and collapsed. It was rebuilt in similar fashion, though not exactly the same, and remains to remind us of a great artist who became a typical 18th century squire.

A Man-Trap
Dorset County Museum

IN DORSET COUNTY Museum there is an extraordinary suit of armour (not now exhibited). Armour is not unusual in museums, but in this case the cap is made of straw bound with split bramble, and the jack or coat of quilted canvas. This equipment was used by deer-hunters on Cranborne chase, and the armour was protection against the quarter-staves of the gamekeepers. Poachers had to tread warily: vicious iron traps could snap a man's leg, and spring-guns could blast him with shot.

Folk-memory is extraordinarily long and even now the issues of hunting and poaching cause emotion to run high. Hunting was restricted to the upper-classes from soon after the Norman Conquest, and the legend of Robin Hood as a Saxon hero challenging the Norman oppressor on behalf of the ordinary people became strongly entrenched. Long after the division between Saxon and Norman had ceased to have any real meaning, it was the landowners who had the monopoly of hunting and in 1671 the property qualification for hunting game was raised to the ownership of land worth £100 per annum.

The definition of what animals, birds and fish constituted game; where and when they might be hunted and by whom; were matters frequently debated in a Parliament whose membership was dominated by substantial landowners. Between 1660 and 1831 there were fifty-four Acts of Parliament dealing with hunting and poaching. Gamekeepers were given extraordinary powers, including from 1693 the right to kill poachers at night, while poachers going armed themselves at night were made subject to the death penalty in 1772. Transportation and imprisonment as well as heavy fines were imposed and many offences could be dealt with by a single justice relying on the evidence of one witness, usually a gamekeeper.

The potential for tyranny and injustice was enormous and the tradition of country people going out to get something for the pot was almost irremovable: resentment, fear and occasional violence were inevitable. The power of gamekeepers was recognised as needing some control by Parliament. In 1711 landowners were limited to one gamekeeper per manor and their names were to be registered with the Clerk of the Peace. From 1784 a certificate had to be issued annually for each gamekeeper at a cost of 10s6d and this regulation was not repealed until 1949. In the Dorset Quarter Sessions Order Books are lists of gamekeepers – nearly two hundred were registered in one period of fourteen years.

The Battle of Chettle Common near Cranborne in 1780 between poachers and gamekeepers was bloody. A gamekeeper was killed, and another had his knee smashed by a swingle normally used for beating hemp. The poachers' leader turned out to be a sergeant of dragoons, but he had a hand cut off by a gamekeeper's cutlass. The sergeant was a popular local figure, and got off with a short prison sentence. He kept his military half-pay and became a game-dealer in London.

- 59 and 60 -
A Fire-back and a Kitchen Range
Dorset County Museum and The Priest's House, Wimborne

THE ARRIVAL OF THE blast-furnace in the 15th century in England led first to cast-iron guns and then to cast-iron fire-backs. As so often happens, advances in military hardware preceded domestic improvements.

Although the mass production of iron was concentrated in fuel-rich areas like the Weald, all over the country there were individual smiths with small bellows-charged furnaces pouring molten iron into moulds to create useful and decorative objects, like this fire-back produced in the early 17th century in Dorchester. When the mediaeval central hearth of a house was moved to a wall with a chimney, the home became much less smoky, but the wall behind the fire needed protection. The fireback provided this, and had the further advantages of reflecting heat back into the room and

showing pleasant decoration when the fire was out.

Cooking on an open fire was limited in scope, and most of the heat was wasted. The traditional roast joint on a turning horizontal spit was only in the province of the better-off, and most people in towns would use the services of a cookshop's ovens to do their baking.

Before 1800 a series of experiments by inventors began the development of kitchen 'ranges' – cast-iron fireboxes with ovens, hobs, boilers, grates and hotplates. Such constructions could often fit into the traditional wide fireplaces. It was even possible to use a spit for the customary roast, although the spit was now vertical and suspended from a 'swing-iron': the meat was held behind a metal screen.

More sophisticated designs crowded upon one another, and the domestic standards of the country rose dramatically. By the end of the 19th century, the 'Sunday roast' was becoming universal. Gas ovens and then electric cookers reduced the demand for ranges, but the invention of the 'Aga' in 1922 revived the idea, and it still flourishes for the 'cognoscenti'.

- 61 -
A Blunderbuss
Dorset County Museum

THERE IS IN DORSET County Museum a small cylinder of brass, with a bell mouth and a long tang at the other end. This latter was clearly intended to be inserted into a wooden stock, which has rotted away – because the gun was retrieved from the site of the wreck of the *Halsewell*.

This ship belonged to the East India Company, and was of 758 tons. She was strongly-built, because East Indiamen had to face the rigours of worldwide trade, through oceans where the natural hazards of extreme weather were made worse by frequent war and endemic piracy.

In early January 1786 *Halsewell* sailed from the Thames bound for Bengal, with a company of 240 passengers and crew. The ship struggled down the Channel through severe storms, and lost her mizenmast completely. It was later reported that some of the crew refused to obey orders and retreated to their hammocks. During the night of 5th January Captain Pierce tried to find shelter in Studland Bay, but the ship became unmanageable in a blizzard of snow. About two o' clock in the morning of 6th January and in pitch darkness

Halsewell crashed into the cliffs between St Albans Head and Anvil Point.

With the force of the waves smashing the ship on to the rocks she soon began to break up. Some of the stronger men managed to scramble on to a ledge in the mouth of a cave, but most of the company including the captain and his two daughters stayed with the ship and were eventually drowned as she broke up.

Some of those on the ledge were washed off, but one managed to climb the 100-foot cliff and ran for help. The Purbeck quarrymen arrived with ropes and hauled up about 70 exhausted sailors. Altogether it was reckoned that 170 people were lost.

Ever since, remnants of the ship and her cargo have been discovered. Soon after the wreck a number of guns and trading items were salvaged and sold at auction. The blunderbuss on show in Dorset County Museum is a typical piece carried in ships, as it was designed to fire a spread of shot against a boarding party or possibly mutineers.

- 62 -
A Coadestone Pillar
Lyme Regis Museum

THIS PILLAR IS A classic example of the products of a factory making artificial stone on the banks of the Thames at Lambeth. The connection with Dorset may seem thin – but the Coade family had come from Lyme Regis. Eleanor, who ran the business very successfully in London, took over a large house above the Cobb called Belmont, which she used increasingly in her later years.

It is extraordinary that this single young woman organised an enterprise in which she had no expertise or experience; employed craftsmen and artists to produce high quality fine art; sold her products very profitably to the upper classes and even royalty – and when she was in her eighties passed on the business to successors who failed to keep it going.

The 'secret' recipe for Coadestone involved the use of previously-fired clay ground fine and mixed with unfired clay, flint, sand and ground glass. The mixture was kneaded together with water to form a paste.

A model of the object to be achieved was made in ordinary clay by the artist, and then covered in plaster to make a mould. Large or complicated designs were moulded in separate pieces. The paste was then pressed into the mould by hand, and allowed to dry. Then the sections were assembled using more water to smooth the joints, making sure that the whole object was hollow to prevent cracking when fired. When dry the product was fired in a very hot kiln for four days, under the expert care of an experienced fireman, whose pay reflected the value of his skill.

All kinds of elaborate stonework were created, and Coadestone statues, monuments, entablatures and decorations are to be found all over Britain. Eleanor's house Belmont survives with plenty of examples, but there are two features well-known to all who visit Dorset. The statue of George III on the Esplanade at Weymouth is one, and the other is the five-legged stag on the Stag Gate on the A31.

- 63 -
Dorset Buttons
Gold Hill Museum, Shaftesbury

DORSET BUTTONY has a strong hold on Dorset folklore and tradition. It was an industry which employed many people for two hundred years, but now it survives only in folk art and craft. Gold Hill Museum in Shaftesbury has a vibrant collection of the most attractive examples, which still inspire with their individual beauty and skilful finish.

Clothes had mostly relied on lacing with leather thongs until the 17th century. A craftsman called Abraham Case came to Shaftesbury in the 1620s and began the manufacture of delicate buttons which seem to have become popular very rapidly. The earliest were conical in shape and were known as 'High Tops'.

The craft consisted in taking a small slim disc of ram's horn, putting a hole in it and sewing linen or other material over it to provide a decorative pattern. The finished buttons were then fixed to paper sheets for sale.

The industry developed on the basis of women and children working in their own homes and taking the buttons at fixed times to a local 'depot' which was the premises of an entrepreneur. He would buy the buttons at whatever was the going rate, and then sell on his stock to merchants at fairs and markets, or take the buttons for resale in London or Bath.

Like most other 'cottage' industries it was 'sweated', in that the rates of pay were low in spite of the great skill and artistry demonstrated. However, it also had the great advantages for the women that they could supplement the family income without leaving their children, and their hours were at their choice. It was reckoned in 1793 that there were 4000 buttoners in the Shaftesbury area alone.

By the 18th century there were depots right across Dorset with the main centres at Shaftesbury and Blandford. The Case family continued to play a big part and they even had a depot for export at Liverpool. The use of metal rings or wire as well as horn provided a cheaper button. As the English population rose, demand continued to increase, until the mid-19th century.

In 1851 a button-making machine was demonstrated at the Great Exhibition at Crystal Palace. Within a few years hand button-making declined drastically. Prices collapsed, and there was widespread distress among the former buttoners. Many people were forced to leave the countryside and look for work in the industrial towns of the North, or indeed to emigrate. Buttony is now just a folk memory.

THE BAD NEWS is, you are very vulnerable to Smallpox, a killer disease. The good news is that it has disappeared from the world – the last known case anywhere was in Somalia in 1977. You are vulnerable because the immunity achieved in earlier generations by infection or inoculation has faded, but there is now no virus to attack you. Sigh of relief!

Smallpox has a long history. Its origins are in prehistory, and it may have been present in Ancient Egypt. It came in epidemics, and had a mortality rate of about 30%, but if you survived an infection you were immunised for life. The drawback of survival was hideous deformity, since the pocks or pustules left 'pockets' or holes. Fashionable Georgian ladies wore little black patches to disguise the ravages.

The traditional hero whose work was heralded as the beginning of the end for the disease was Dr Edward Jenner, the London physician who experimented with vaccination in the late 18th century. He was rewarded with huge sums of money by a grateful House of Commons, and in most reference works he is given sole credit. This is unjust, because although he did all that was said, he was forestalled by twenty years by a small Dorset farmer.

Benjamin Jesty was born in 1736, the son of a Yetminster butcher. He married Elizabeth Notley, and took on Upbury Farm in the High Street next to the churchyard at Yetminster. At some time he contracted cowpox, a comparatively mild disease which was quite usual in the farming community. Country people were already aware that having cowpox gave you a good chance that you would not be infected by the more serious smallpox.

When the dreaded smallpox arrived in Yetminster in 1774, Jesty decided to take drastic action to protect his wife and two sons. He took them to visit a neighbouring farm where there was a cow infected with cowpox. He took an old darning needle, dipped it into the pus oozing from the cow's sores, and then scratched the skins of his family with the fearsome implement. All three contracted cowpox: the two boys quite mildly, though Mrs Jesty's

condition gave cause for concern. Jesty's neighbours were horrified, but the family did not catch smallpox.

Twenty years later, the surgeon Edward Jenner carried out similar experiments, and coined the word 'vaccine' from the Latin 'vacca' – a cow. Reports of his work were published, and the idea

(Sacred)
To the Memory
OF
Benjm Jesty (of Downshay)
who departed this Life,
April 16th 1816.
aged 79 Years.

He was born at Yetminster in this
County, and was an upright honest
Man: particularly noted for having
been the first Person (known) that
introduced the Cow Pox
by Inoculation, and who from
his great strength of mind made the
Experiment from the (Cow) on
his Wife and two Sons in the Year 1774.

Sacred
To the Memory
of
ELIZABETH JESTY
Relict of the late BENJ: JEST
of Downshay who Departed this li
Jan: 8th 1824
Aged 84 Years.

The Time we have allotted here
We highly ought to prize,
And strive to make Salvation sure
Ere Death doth close our eyes.

began to spread. The traditional reaction was to be expected: introducing animal disease into human beings was unnatural, sinful and to be reviled. Nevertheless, his successful experiments were rewarded by official recognition and he was awarded prizes totalling £30,000 (many millions today). Gradually vaccination reduced and finally eliminated smallpox. Until the mid-twentieth century many adults bore the permanent small scar left by the operation.

Meanwhile Benjamin Jesty continued quietly farming, moving to Downshay Manor Farm near Worth Matravers in Purbeck in 1797. Early attempts to have his initiative recognised failed, largely through his own lack of co-operation, but in 1805 this obscure Dorset farmer's achievement of thirty years before was finally given official notice: but no financial award was made! He went on farming until his death in 1816.

The Tarleton Helmet 1797
The Keep Military Museum, Dorchester

THERE IS A STRONG element of swashbuckling in this piece of cavalry headgear. It was a style favoured by a British hero of the American Revolutionary War, Banastre Tarleton. The British lost the war in 1782, but Tarleton's exploits as an independent commander of light dragoons brought him fame, the discarded mistress of the Prince of Wales, and a portrait (with the helmet) painted by Sir Joshua Reynolds. The helmet caught on.

A few years later the French had their Revolution and chopped off the heads of their King and Queen. The consequent horror of the other European monarchs led to war. There was a distinct possibility that the failure of the Allies to defeat the French could lead to an invasion of England, and the coastal counties began to take defensive measures.

In 1794 the Dorset Volunteer Rangers were formed. They were light cavalry, and wore a green uniform and helmet inspired by Banastre Tarleton. The Rangers provided their own horses and bridles, paid for their uniforms and sabres, and the officers had their portraits painted by William Beech. The officers were mainly gentry, and the other ranks were better-off farmers.

The first Field-Day was held at Pound-bury in June 1794, but soon afterwards the Saturday parades were suspended until after harvest and sheep shearing. First things first! Parades resumed in the spring of 1795. Being late on parade was expensive: the fine was a shilling, equivalent to a day's wage for a farm labourer.

At this time the officers were employed in making returns of the cattle, grain, potatoes, flax and hay in the county – part of the extensive preparation for meeting an invasion. The returns were incorporated in a series of plans and instructions set out by the magistrates' clerks and issued to the constables and other officials across the county. When the emergency was over (the French never came) these plans were filed carefully in the County Records. They were taken out and examined 150 years later when Hitler threatened to attack.

Towns and villages across Dorset raised their own companies of foot-soldiers, such as the Puddletown Volunteer Light Infantry. The shortage of muskets was met in 1804 by the issue of pikes, newly refurbished, sharpened and repainted after 200 years storage in church towers since the threat of the Spanish Armada. They were put back later, and it is said that some of the early Home Guard units in 1940 used them for drill!

The officers of the Volunteer Infantry were usually farmers or shop-keepers. The Infantry did not have the prestige of the Cavalry, but they paraded regularly and attempted strict discipline, with fines for talking in the ranks or having a dirty musket. Attendance was rewarded with the King's shilling – and after parade the alehouse was open.

The Evershot and Sydling Light Infantry were disbanded in disgrace. They were ordered to march to a Field-Day, but refused because it was raining and they didn't want to spoil their new uniforms. The General was not amused.

The Hardy Monument

Near Portesham

AS NELSON LAY dying at the Battle of Trafalgar he is said to have murmured to his old friend the Captain of HMS *Victory* "'Kiss me, Hardy".

Hardy is commemorated by a great tower built on the hill above Portesham and overlooking Lyme Bay. The monument was built in 1844 from local subscriptions, in memory of Vice-Admiral Sir Thomas Masterman Hardy, Flag-Captain to Admiral Lord Nelson at the Battle of Trafalgar. The stone tower is 72 feet high, and there is an internal winding staircase to a viewing platform which gives spectacular panoramic views of the coast and countryside.

Hardy was born in 1769, either in Portesham or Martinstown: sources vary. He first went to sea at the age of twelve, serving with Captain Roberts of Burton Bradstock. In the next few years his time was divided between sea-service and education at Milton Abbey. In 1790 he rejoined the Royal Navy as Midshipman under Captain Hood of Netherbury.

Service in various ships led to promotion as Lieutenant in 1793, and he joined Nelson's squadron in the Mediterranean. Adventures followed, including six weeks as a prisoner of the French, but in 1797 he was promoted to Commander as captain of *Mutine,* a brig of 16 guns. A year later, after the great Battle of the Nile he was given *Vanguard* (74) as Flag-Captain to Admiral Nelson.

He came home in 1799, arriving at the King's Arms in Dorchester on Christmas Eve. Further service with Nelson took him to the Baltic and the Battle of Copenhagen in 1801. Appointment to *Victory* in 1803 as Nelson's Flag-Captain once more, led him to the Battle of Trafalgar in 1805. The French Emperor Napoleon had gathered a great fleet of French and Spanish battleships at Cadiz on the south-west coast of Spain. His intention was to defeat the Royal Navy and to escort a French invasion force across the English Channel. This was to be the final conquest of Britain in a war which had already lasted more than ten years.

Admiral Lord Nelson had out-manoeuvred the French Admiral Villeneuve in a thrilling chase across to the West Indies, and now the British fleet patrolled up and down the Spanish coast waiting for the enemy to emerge.

When they did come out in October 1805 Nelson, standing alongside Captain Thomas Hardy in *Victory,* broke their line with two squadrons. It was 27 ships against 33, but the superior gunnery and training of the Royal Navy carried the day. Two-thirds of the French and Spanish ships were sunk or captured. Nelson died in the battle, but never again did Britain fear invasion – until 1940.

For his distinguished service in the battle Hardy was awarded a baronetcy. In 1807 he married Anne Berkeley and had three daughters. He continued his naval career mostly at sea, reaching the rank of Vice-Admiral. His final appointment was as Governor of Greenwich Hospital for naval pensioners, and he died there in 1839. When Trafalgar Square and Nelson's Column were created in the early 1840s, the Dorset gentry felt that their local hero should be remembered too. The hat was passed round, and Hardy's Monument was built.

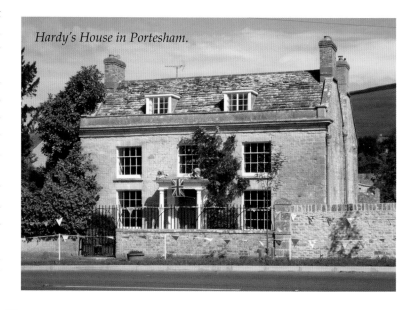

Hardy's House in Portesham.

A Coaching Inn Bell
Dorchester County Museum

PASSENGER COACHES for the public developed during the 18th century. Stages of about ten to fifteen miles had existed for many years, for the postboys on horseback, with inns acting as depots for the supply of fresh horses. The coaching inns in Dorchester were The King's Arms and the Antelope in the centre of town, and the White Hart at the foot of High East Street. The arches into the inn-yards are still there at both King's Arms and Antelope.

Early coaches were unsprung, with beam axles bolted to the coach frame. Feeling every bump, ridge and pothole, passengers would arrive at the inn tired, sore, hungry and thirsty – and mine host would be delighted to meet every requirement at a price. However, as road surfaces improved it became possible to make

The Antelope, Dorchester
This old Bell was originally fixed in the Courtyard of this House and was rung to give warning to passengers of the impending departure of Coaches

lighter coaches with thinner wheels, and in 1784 John Palmer of Bath introduced the first Mail Coach – with springs.

Soon Royal Mail coaches were operating on all the good turnpiked roads, and lines from east, west and north passed through Dorchester. The Royal Mail did not pay tolls, and at the sound of the guard's posthorn the gates were hurriedly opened as the coach and four galloped through. For the passengers there was one slight disadvantage: the new springs were not damped, and there were no shock-absorbers. The result could be a continuous wave-like motion, and passengers could be feeling sea-sick for most of the journey.

The mail coaches were painted deep maroon and black with red wheels, and made a pretty sight as they dashed through the countryside at ten miles an hour. By the 1830s the services had reached their peak, and coaches were a familiar part of the Dorset daily routine.

It requires a little imagination to see the busy scene: the Royal Mail from London clattering up the cobbles of High East Street, the driver whipping the tired horses up the hill and the guard blowing furiously on his posthorn to warn the ostlers and the waiters at the King's Arms to be ready. The coach would swing widely to the left, and then round to the right and under the arch, with the outside passengers ducking to save their heads. Almost before the coach stopped the horses would be unharnessed and four fresh ones buckled in. Five minutes were allowed for the changeover. The bell on the wall would be rung furiously to warn passengers of impending departure, and then the horn was blown again and the coach was off, under the arch and away up High West Street.

Timing for the Royal Mail had to be very exact. On a coach the guard sitting on top at the back held a timepiece like a clock in a leather pouch. This was carefully adjusted so that it would lose nine minutes on the run from London to Dorchester, thus allowing for the time difference measured by the sun.

All this came to an end after the railway arrived in 1847. The first Christmas cards were sent about the same time. Is it a coincidence that mail coaches are a popular nostalgic design for cards even now?

The Antelope Inn.

Mary Anning's 'Fossil Extractor'
Lyme Regis Museum

THIS SIMPLE HAND tool has been the symbol of the life of a remarkable woman. However, recent research has shown that its importance lies only in tradition – the implement is really a late-19th century British Army entrenching tool! The news does not diminish her reputation.

Mary Anning (1799-1847) was the daughter of a cabinet-maker in Lyme Regis, and grew up in poor circumstances. She learned to read and write at Sunday school, and by the age of eleven was already taking an interest in the secondary family trade of finding fossils to sell to tourists.

The cliffs at Lyme Regis are often unstable, and winter rains can cause landslides. The Jurassic layers of limestone and shale break down to reveal fossils of ancient animals. By the time of Mary Anning there was vigorous interest in fossils, developing gradually from curiosity to scientific study. The French Wars restricted continental travel for the better-off, and tourists began to explore their own country. The annual visits to Weymouth by the Royal Family encouraged visitors to go a little further along the coast to Lyme Regis, and the little town expanded to meet their needs.

Mary's father was a great collector of fossils, and a table was set up outside their house for display and sale. He died in 1810, but in 1811 her brother found the four-foot skull of what was later called the 'Ichthyosaurus'. Mary aged eleven found the rest of the skeleton a few months later, and a gentleman paid the family £23.00 for it – nearly a year's wages for a working man.

This find and others caused considerable excitement in the scientific community, since these animals were unknown in modern times, and the apparent age of the fossils argued against the current belief in the Biblical age of the Earth. Mary continued her searches, and sold many of her finds, mainly ammonites and belemnite shells, for small sums. The family continued poor, and in 1820 a wealthy and sympathetic collector auctioned his stock and gave them some of the proceeds.

The work of collection could be dangerous, as landslides and

cliff falls were common. On one occasion in 1833 Mary narrowly escaped death, when her dog 'Tray' was killed in front of her by falling rocks. The work went on, and geologists in Europe and America became aware of this extraordinary woman, who read scientific papers whenever she could get hold of them, but never produced her own.

She died of cancer aged 47, but her fame has survived, in spite of the fact that what was thought to be her most useful tool, the 'Fossil Extractor', is not what it seems.

The Red Post

On the A31 5 miles west of Wimborne

A SIGNPOST PAINTED red stands out and is immediately a matter of curiosity. Tales will be told based on gory suppositions of gibbets, but the explanation of this one seems most likely to boil down to the illiteracy of lower-grade officers of the law!

In the early 19th century criminals sentenced in Dorchester to transportation to Australia were required to walk to Portsmouth for embarkation. The guards accompanying a batch of transportees would need to know where to stop overnight, and there was a convenient barn near Winterborne Tomson. Because guards might not be able to read, the turning-off point was made clear by bright red paint. A post in the middle of the barn was a useful fixture for the chains binding the prisoners.

Transportation was developed from the late 17th century as a penalty which was severe, but allowed convicts their lives. Until the American Revolution prisoners were sent to Virginia, but with the first settlements in Australia there was a new opportunity to punish and at the same time to provide the new colonies with cheap labour.

Men and women were sentenced to transportation for seven or fourteen years, or for life. In the 1840s an average of seventeen prisoners a year were transported by Dorset magistrates, and more by judges. The most notorious case was that of the Tolpuddle Martyrs, the trade unionists punished for swearing an illegal oath in 1834. The publicity inspired by this event helped to swing public opinion against transportation, and in 1857 the system was abolished. Dorset magistrates were still enthusiastically transporting housebreakers when the last convict ship sailed: at Easter 1857 William Bartlett was given seven years.

- 70 -
Dorchester Town Pump
Cornhill, Dorchester

THE TOWN PUMP in Dorchester is a monument. It commemorates the efforts of a municipality in a pre-industrial age to provide a public amenity that was also a dignified and attractive feature – and it is this latter quality that ensures its survival.

Roman Dorchester had enjoyed a public water supply, provided by an aqueduct 15 kilometres long, though it was abandoned, and the town reverted to wells and water-carriers for the next 1800 years. There was a town well halfway-down South Street, but in 1784 the market house known as the 'Cupola' at Cornhill was pulled down, and on its site the present Town Pump was built. There were many private wells, but this well with a lever-operated pump was open to all, and much used.

An increasing population meant a greater problem of waste-disposal, which was dealt with in the traditional way by digging more and more cesspits. These drained into the ground from which the wells drew their water, and by 1850 the Public Health of towns was causing great concern. The cholera outbreak in Fordington in 1854 concentrated minds in Dorchester, and it was clear that a supply of clean water together with a system of sewerage was necessary.

In 1860 a deep well was dug just off the Bridport Road, together with a covered reservoir. Distribution through mains across the town cost the Borough £4300, and piped water became available to houses at a planned rate of two pence (less than 1p) per week per house. Sewers discharged raw effluent into the River Frome at Louds Mill, until a sewage farm was built in 1904.

The Town Pump remained as an admired design feature. Its principal use today is as a meeting place for tours of the town, and a focus for town festivities.

- 71 -
The White Horse
Osmington

CARVED ON A CHALKY slope facing south near the village of Osmington is a huge white horse with a bewigged rider. There is some doubt as to exactly when and by whom it was carved, but the rider is King George III, and the most likely date is the first decade of the 19th century. As the inscription on his statue on Weymouth Esplanade clearly states, the inhabitants of the town were grateful for the King's patronage: and the hill-figure may well have been made in the same spirit.

Before 1750 Weymouth was a small fishing port with some coastal and European trade. With better roads the aristocracy began to find their way from Bath to Dorset, to sample the medicinal qualities of sea-water. At the end of the 18th century the annual visits of George III and his large family to Gloucester Lodge on Weymouth front greatly helped the fashion.

Inevitably the town developed to meet the demands of the clientele. Lodging-houses, hotels, bathing-houses, bathing-machines, assembly-rooms and fashionable shops proliferated. It was boom-time in Weymouth. Rows of houses gradually extended along the sea-front, with names redolent of the Court and the aristocracy – Chesterfield Place, Charlotte Row, Clarence Buildings. The Esplanade built in the 1780s was extended in 1805 as far as the harbour mouth. Where previously the beach had been at the back of the town and used as a dump for unwanted refuse, now it was the main centre of activity – at least during the summer months.

If new facilities such as the Theatre and the Library palled in their attraction, the visitors were offered excursions: to Radipole for tea and biscuits at the sign of the 'Honest Man', or to Lulworth by boat where passengers could be met by carriages for the return; or even to Portland by ferry, which charged one penny for foot passengers rising to three shillings and sixpence for a coach. Local visiting in Weymouth was made more attractive by the provision of sedan-chairs costing a shilling, or one shilling and sixpence if you wanted to cross the bridge.

Even when the Royal Family ceased to come, the fashion continued. Fifty years later, when the railway came, Weymouth received an immense impetus from a middle-class invasion. Fifty years later still the rising wages of the workers meant that a week by the seaside was possible and desirable, and this too was accentuated by the motor-coach or charabanc. Fifty years on again, and post-war cheap motoring meant further boom-time but then came cheap flying – and some of the holidaymakers went abroad. But not all!

The grateful Inhabitants To GEORGE THE THIRD On His entering the 50th Year Of His REIGN.

- 72 -
A Smuggler's Headstone
Wyke Regis Churchyard

EIGHTEENTH CENTURY Dorset was a hotbed of crime. Smuggling was rife, and every section of society was tinged with it. Some parts of the county were dominated by smuggling, particularly the coastal villages. Reading the records – as opposed to hearing the romantic stories – one is reminded more of the *Mafia* in Sicily than the peaceful English countryside.

In a period when English worldwide trade was expanding, most of that trade was accruing to London, Bristol and Liverpool. Apart from fishing, maritime business in Poole, Weymouth, Bridport and Lyme Regis was stagnating. The imposition of heavy import duties, particularly on luxury items, provided an opportunity for adventurers willing to take physical and financial risks in search of great rewards – and they set to with a will. How the money rolled in!

In the hours of darkness, and sometimes in brazen broad daylight, contraband goods were off-loaded from luggers into small boats or on to rafts. When the few Customs men were elsewhere, the boats would be run ashore on the many convenient beaches. The beaches of Studland Bay were popular: the village was isolated. The rafts carrying kegs of spirits could be piled with heavy stones and sunk for later retrieval. Large gangs of men were recruited to load packhorses and carts, which were escorted along ancient tracks in the hills to wholesale customers throughout the country. Even during the Saturday Market at Wareham it was not unusual to see a line of packhorses and wagons escorted through by the smugglers.

French brandy was favourite in the early days, but tea (then very expensive) and tobacco caught up. The possibilities were endless – rum, linen, silks, soap and glassware and much else. Most came via the Channel Islands, which, though British, were not subject to the duties. Some of the more enterprising spirits among the smugglers became big-businessmen, eventually turning to legitimate trade and becoming gentlemen with their own estates – Isaac Gulliver is the prime example.

Custom House, Weymouth.

Why did the authorities not clamp down? There were two main reasons: to provide an effective Preventive Service would have required a huge investment in patrol ships and staff to cover the long coastline; and the authorities themselves were the Justices of the Peace – among the gentry who indulged themselves in the smuggled goods. As it was, the Customs vessels failed to catch the luggers, the cliff watchers failed to see the landings, the smugglers won the pitched battles with the Preventive officers, and smugglers brought to trial were pronounced Not Guilty by juries who were sympathetic, bribed or intimidated.

Sometimes the smugglers were unlucky, as in the case of William Lewis, whose headstone in Wyke Regis churchyard indicates that he was killed by a shot from the *Pygmy* Preventive schooner in 1822. Quite often the 'Preventives' came off worst and several were murdered. In any case smuggling involved violence and threats to law-abiding people, and the abolition of Customs Duties by William Gladstone in the 1850s put an end to a nasty and very unromantic activity.

West Bay - a landing place for contraband.

The Tolpuddle Martyrs Poster 1834
Dorset County Museum

IN 1834 THE Dorset landowners were apprehensive. A few years earlier the 'Captain Swing' riots by agricultural labourers demanding better wages and conditions had frightened the gentry and the farmers. The formation of trade unions, and especially national trade unions of labourers, threatened to upset the traditional relationship between master and man. In particular, if farmers were forced to pay higher wages, then they could not pay higher rents to landowners, whose wealth and way of life would be endangered.

Rather naïve attempts to persuade landowner-magistrates to support them against the farmers were made by the labourers on the farms around Tolpuddle, a village six miles from Dorchester. Promises of support from the parson were not kept. The labourers of Tolpuddle, desperate to feed their families, secretly formed a branch of the Grand National Consolidated Trades Union, and met in a cottage still standing today.

A leading county magistrate, James Frampton of Moreton, became alarmed. Threatened in the earlier riots, and having been in Paris as a young man at the time of the French Revolution, he clearly expected the 'secret' trade union to be the precursor of bloody rebellion. He wrote to the rather indolent Home Secretary, Lord Melbourne, asking for advice. Correspondence eventually elicited the suggestion that if the union members were taking secret oaths, then they might be prosecuted under a war-time Act of 1797 designed to combat naval mutinies.

Accordingly, Frampton secured the necessary evidence from an

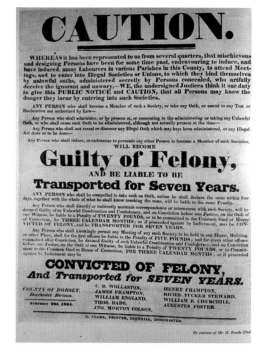

informer, and posted bills in Tolpuddle warning that secret oaths were criminal. Almost immediately he organised the arrest of six labourers. They were taken to Dorchester, examined by the Recorder of Dorchester Sir Charles Wollaston in his own house (still standing near Waitrose), and committed in custody.

The trial, in what is now called The Old Crown Court, was held by a newly-appointed judge, Mr Baron Williams. The result of the trial was never in doubt. In their ignorance of the law, the labourers, led by George Loveless, had sworn a secret oath to keep the rules of the union, and this was illegal. The real issue was trade unionism and all involved knew it – though Loveless was convinced that he and the others had been picked on because they were Methodists and therefore specially obnoxious to land-owning Anglicans.

Judge Williams passed the sentence allowed by law, and expected of him by those determined to stamp out associations of work-people. Seven years transportation to the penal colonies of Australia was not seen by them as unduly harsh. A few years later, following widespread protest, the labourers were brought back to England.

The tribulations of the Tolpuddle Martyrs have become an icon of trade union history. The episode did not reflect well on the Dorset magistracy, but the fears of a group of people who could see their comfortable and secure lives disintegrating in the face of apparent mob-rule can be understood, even if their actions cannot be condoned.

- 74 -
Bishop's Kiln
Above Abbotsbury

ON THE ROAD DOWN to Abbotsbury from the Hardy Monument is small lay-by known as the 'Bishop's Kiln'. It is ideal for picnics and as a viewpoint – but how did it come to be there? It is a monument to the enormous efforts of farmers to improve their land and crops.

As the population of England increased from the 16th century, so did the demand for food; prices rose, and naturally farmers looked for better yields so that they could take advantage. All kinds of ideas were tried, but one which improved fertility using local materials developed rapidly. This was the burning of limestone rock to make quicklime, which when slaked and spread on the fields acted as a useful fertiliser.

The limestone of Dorset was plentiful, and many farmers constructed their own kilns cutting into hillsides, and building with brick and stone. There were different shapes, but basically a kiln was an upside-down cone with an iron grill at the bottom. Limestone and chalk were piled in on top of coal and 'culm' (a mixture of coal-dust), and fire was applied. As the kiln baked so the quicklime fell through the grill, to be collected in lumps which were heaped at corners of fields to be scattered as they were slaked by the rain.

Limekilns are to be found all over Dorset – more than two hundred have been recognised. Through the 18th and 19th centuries the process continued. Lime was also a building-mortar – indeed much was used in the construction of Corfe Castle in the 13th century. When slaked the resulting liquid could be used for white-washing walls. The ash from the kilns made a good covering for the bare-earth floors of cottages.

Suddenly technological change caught up once more. In the late 19th century, new and more effective fertilisers became available – natural ones like South American Guano, and chemical ones as well. Portland cement took the place of lime mortar, and the kilns were left to go cold.

A Water-Meadow Sluice
River Frome, Dorchester

BY THE EARLY 17th century the demand for consumer goods in England and Europe had grown dramatically. Rising prices, the development of world-wide trade, increasing populations with hungry mouths and backs to clothe – all provided incentives for producers to get more out the land. Books were published with good ideas, and one idea which may have come from Holland via Cambridgeshire was the water-meadow.

If the meadows could be irrigated by a controlled system, then the annual crop of grass and hay could be vastly increased. The problem was how to provide enough water early in the year to encourage early growth and to raise the earth-temperature, and then for it to be drained off rapidly to prevent flooding and allow grazing.

A series of channels, sluices and ditches had to be carefully planned – it could not casually evolve. Engineers were required to establish diversion of streams, the construction of 'head mains', the excavation of shallow channels and of the drains which would allow the water to return to the natural stream, and the building of 'hatches' to control the flow.

A successful system meant early grazing for sheep, large crops of hay, and then grazing of cattle on the aftermath. Chalk country was best for the scheme, and the remains of water-meadows can be seen all round Dorchester.

Once in place a team of craftsmen was required to operate the system. The leading crewman was called a 'Drowner', and it was his responsibility to fill the head main from the stream, and then by controlling the hatches to allow just the right amount of water to run along the channels. The early hatches were wooden and rather primitive, but later on they were made of cast iron and operated with winding gear. The firm of Hossey and Galpin in Dorchester began to make iron hatches in 1811, and their names can still be seen on the machinery.

During the winter the work of the 'crew' consisted of clearing weed and rubbish from the channels. Then the hatches could be adjusted to allow a flow: the ideal was for the water to enter slowly and to be drained off rapidly – 'in at a trot and out at a gallop'! The initial trickle was designed to flow through the roots of spring growth, to warm and protect from frosts. The sheep could then munch on the new grass from late February to late April, before a 'floating' to help the hay crop. The sheep population grew rapidly.

By the 1880s the emphasis was changing towards cattle, cereals and cattle fodder as it became possible to pipe water to the upland pastures. Australia and New Zealand were competing successfully with English sheep, and the use of fertilisers began to make the water-meadows unnecessary. New heavy farm machinery which could not be turned on the 20-yard 'panes' between the channels completed the demise, particularly after the Second World War.

Water-meadow sluice winding gear.

A Fish Hook
Poole Museum

THIS IS NO ORDINARY fish hook. It is a surviving symbol of an extraordinary industry and trade on which rose the fortunes of the Borough of Poole.

The word is cod. Other take-away meals have risen to tempt the palate, but the humble cod-and-chips is still a succulent dish for most people. And yet there is a paradox: it was only as the great trade between Poole and the Newfoundland fisheries declined, that new technology in storage and preservation made street-corner fish-and-chips a staple diet in Britain.

The Newfoundland Banks where huge codfish teemed became known to Europeans only gradually, as the early explorers of the New World sailed tentatively across the vast Atlantic Ocean in the sixteenth century. As the Danes came to dominate the Icelandic waters in the distant north, so the English fishermen found new potential far across the Western Seas.

Fishing with hook-and-line from small wooden sailing-ships along dangerous shores and in stormy waters, two thousand miles from home, landing in hostile and inhospitable country to process the catch: the conditions suggest that the rewards of the trade must have been great. They were – but only for the businessmen who financed the ventures.

On arrival on the Grand Banks, the Dorset fishermen had first to stock up with bait. Rotting fish and dead puffins could be bought from the "overstayers" – men who spent the winter months in squalid huts on the beaches. With the hooks baited then the fish had to be found – often very easy in the early days when seamen recalled sailing through huge shoals. Sometimes large barrels were strapped to the sides of the ships, and men in them could more easily control the long lines with the fearsome hooks.

When the hold was full, the catch was landed, and teams of men would cut off their heads, split and gut the fish and spread salt over them. Laid out on boards the cod were left to dry, while the ships sailed again for more fish harvest. At the end of the season when the weather grew worse, the fleet would head back across the Atlantic with the holds full of stacked dried cod. With them would also go train-oil, squeezed from the cod-livers. It fetched 2 pence a pint and was used in lamps, cloth-making, leather and soap. Any spare space might be taken up with furs from beaver, fox and seal.

Returning ships did not come straight back to Poole. The countries around the Mediterranean provided the best market for all these goods, and they specially enjoyed the dried cod. The customers paid in cash, the captains bought salt for the next voyage and came home to make the ship-owners rich. A merchant aristocracy built great houses in and around Poole, and some made the transition to gentry.

Recruitment of fishermen was the biggest problem. When times were good and employment ashore plentiful, few men would relish the hard and dangerous life on the Grand Banks. The pay was small, and rascally captains would cheat their men. Only when jobs were very scarce could full crews be found, and then only by liaising with the Poor Law Overseers trying to offload the paupers from their lists to be relieved by the parish.

An Election Poster 1831
Dorset History Centre

IN THE STRUGGLE FOR Parliamentary Reform in the 1830s broadly the Whigs were all for change and the Tories for keeping the status quo. The Whigs railed about the corruption and unfair representation, and the Tories said that giving more seats in the House of Commons to the North would hand power to the factory owners and ruin the interest of farmers and landowners.

Contested elections were quite rare. Most seats were filled by agreement between local gentry, because until the introduction of the Secret Ballot in 1874 voters could be bribed, and this was expensive. It was therefore very unusual when there were two elections in Dorset within a few months in 1831.

Since the beginnings of Parliament in the 13th century each county had elected two Members, and each borough had elected two Members. The County Members were usually from the leading aristocratic and gentle families. By the early 19th century most boroughs also elected local gentry, under the influence of landowners like the Earl of Shaftesbury. The General Election of May 1831 took place in the furore of the Bill for Parliamentary Reform. Of the three candidates for the two Dorset seats, Mr Portman was a Whig Reformer, Mr Bankes was a Tory and anti-Reform, and Mr Calcraft had been a Tory government minister but had now changed his mind and supported Reform. Portman and Calcraft, both Reformers, were elected.

Dorsetshire Freeholders.

Important Questions?

1st.---Is Dorsetshire so poor in Men of Talent and Worth, that we must needs have an Irishman to represent the County?

2ndly.---Is Mr. PONSONBY, being closely entangled with Roman Catholic connexions, likely to strenuously protect our Interests as Protestants?

3rdly.---Will Mr. PONSONBY be a fit Member for an Agricultural County, when he consents to give Householders of £10 per Annum in Towns a Vote for Representatives in Parliament, but denies the same Privilege to Farmers renting £50 per Ann. in the Country?

4thly.---Are a widely scattered rural Population to be ruled by a few self-elected Committees in two or three of the principal Towns?

5thly.---Is it wise to depute Mr. PONSONBY to speak for us in the House of Commons, where he has hitherto never given more than a silent Vote?

6thly.---Will the Independent Freeholders of this County submit to such an everlasting disgrace?

A RUSTIC FREEHOLDER.

In early September Calcraft committed suicide – it was thought he had been severely affected by the criticism launched at him as a 'turncoat'. A by-election was called.

The Whigs proposed Mr Ponsonby, who was one of the MPs for Poole. Mr Bankes refused to stand again, and Lord Ashley was nominated by the Tories. He too was already an MP – for Dorchester. Lord Ashley made his campaign headquarters at the Kings Arms, convenient for the Hustings raised on Poundbury hillfort, where voting took place over the next eighteen days.

The High Sheriff began proceedings by asking for a show of hands among the voters. He declared that Mr Ponsonby had won, but this was challenged and the voters filed by to register their votes. Each one had to show that he held land in Dorset to the value of forty shillings per year. Large crowds attended, most of them having no right to vote at all. Every day the candidates made speeches at the hustings, and more votes were taken. Lord Ashley made himself very busy, entertaining voters at hostelries across West Dorset. Pamphlets and posters, some of them scurrilous, were published by both sides. After a race-meeting near Dorchester, two hundred men rode into the town and paraded outside the Kings Arms, cheering and shouting in support of Ashley.

On 17th October the final count was taken, and Lord Ashley

declared the winner, by 36 votes. The rival crowds on Poundbury (most of them non-voters) came to blows, and the Yeomanry Cavalry were summoned to restore order. Riots followed at Blandford and Sherborne, where the windows of Sherborne Castle were broken. On November 5th effigies of Ashley were burnt instead of guys.

Ashley was left to count the very high cost of his entertainment campaign – but as the Earl of Shaftesbury he went on to become one of the great social reformers of the 19th century. As it was, his anti-reform victory made no difference: Parliament passed the Great Reform Act in 1832.

TO THE
GENTRY, CLERGY,
AND
Freeholders
OF THE COUNTY OF
DORSET.

GENTLEMEN,

IT is impossible for me to describe in adequate terms my sense of your exertions, and the extent of my gratitude.

When I consider how short a Notice was given of my intentions, and compare it with the long previous Canvass of my Antagonist, I feel assured, that nothing but general energy and unwearied individual zeal, could have enabled me ultimately to Triumph, or even for a while to maintain an Opposition.

The Contest has been one of unexampled vigour, and almost of unexampled duration; yet, few Contests, I rejoice to say, have been less marked by personal or social conflict; so far as I myself am concerned, I shall speedily forget whatever there may have been of hostility in the actions or language of my Opponents; and shall endeavour to fulfil those duties which my Friends have imposed upon me, not for their exclusive advantage, but for the benefit of the County at large.

When I first ventured to address you at the outset of the Election, I expressed a wish " to identify my cause with the cause of the Constitution;" I may now assume that my wishes were your's, and that I, as your Representative, may declare your firm adherence to those great principles which inspirit and regulate our glorious Constitution in Church and State.

To the discharge of my duties as a County Member, I cannot yet bring the results of experience; but the deficiency shall be supplied by industry and good will. My Friends, I will avow, have a claim upon my gratitude as well as upon my services, and every Constituent may demand, and shall receive my utmost assistance in his public business.

I shall avail myself of the earliest opportunity to wait on you personally, and express those thanks to which you are so justly entitled, and which I so deeply feel.

I am, GENTLEMEN,
Your most obedient humble Servant,
ASHLEY.

DORCHESTER, October 18, 1831.

Weston, Simonds, and Sydenham, Chronicle Office, Dorchester.

A Bridge Warning
Sturminster Newton

BRIDGES ARE ROMANTIC, fascinating and sometimes inspiring – but every bridge is an indication of economic activity. Early bridges were of timber, which rotted, and when times were better and trade sufficient, timber was replaced with stone. In many places in Dorset there are stone bridges first built in the later Middle Ages, and repaired, widened, lengthened and strengthened many times since.

From the 16th century the repair of roads and bridges became the responsibility of the parishes through which they ran. Sometimes a bridge would cross a river which was the boundary between parishes, or even counties. Naturally the ratepayers on either side were reluctant to pay and disputes could delay repairs. Appeal would be made to the county magistrates who would send a justice to decide. Inter-county issues were more difficult, and

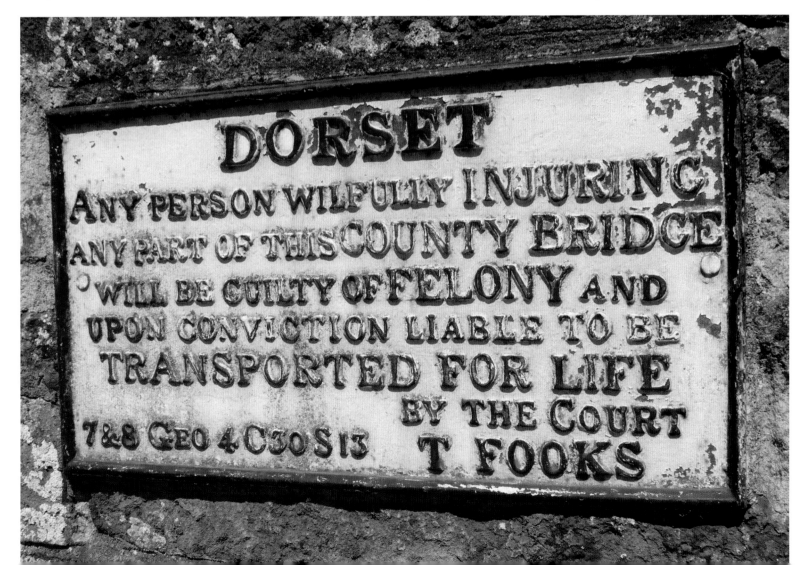

sometimes a broken bridge would remain for years. It did happen that one half of a bridge would be repaired while the other half was left in ruins, to the chagrin of road users.

Soon after the twin towns of Weymouth and Melcombe Regis were joined by Act of Parliament in 1571, they were joined by a wooden bridge. It had a lifting section to allow ships to pass

Julian Bridge, Wimborne.

up the harbour to be beached for hull-cleaning. Over the centuries several rebuildings in stone followed, with the most recent having been created with the help of the citizens of Weymouth Massachusetts.

In the 1630s the Dorset Justices were faced with a huge demand for bridge repairs across the county. The Five Bridges near Sherborne, Tarrant Crawford Bridge, Canford Bridge and Julian Bridge at Wimborne were all falling down and trade was being hindered. Very large sums of money were demanded in rates, and the work was completed in time for the Civil War!

Social unrest after the Napoleonic Wars in the early 19th century led to concern that disaffected workers might try to upset trade by bridge-breaking, and the Clerk of the Peace had cast-iron notices placed on many bridges warning miscreants that they might find themselves breaking stones in Australia. Some of these plates survive; for example at Sturminster Newton, and Grey's Bridge at Dorchester. Later in the Victorian period the introduction of steam traction-engines for farm haulage caused further notices warning that bridges could not stand the huge weight of such vehicles. Altogether the magistrates of the county were doubtless glad to hand over responsibility for Roads and Bridges to the newly-formed County Council in 1889.

A Model Brewery
Dorset County Museum

THE USE OF BARLEY-malt to create a pleasant and intoxicating liquor is extremely ancient and was practised in Dorset from at least the Bronze Age. Domestic brewing has never died out, but brewing for sale has gone through many changes and adaptations, and was an early candidate for industrialisation.

The alehouse which sold its own product was familiar in every village and in the streets of towns in mediaeval England. 'Good ale is meat, drink and cloth' ran the proverb. Enterprising brewers supplied landlords who lacked the equipment. By the mid-sixteenth century problems of popular disorder (consequent on economic and social issues) led to Parliament passing an Act for the licensing of alehouses. Licences were to be issued by magistrates only to landlords who maintained well-ordered premises, and miscreant alehousekeepers were to be 'suppressed'.

In 1577 the government of Queen Elizabeth I ordered a survey of all alehouses and taverns. The authorities in Dorset reported that there were 209 alehouses in the county, which was probably an underestimate since it is known that there were many unlicensed – and therefore illegal – premises. The popular name for an ale-seller was 'tippler'.

Traditionally someone who had brewed a quantity of ale would plant a pole outside his house with a bush hanging from it to announce that he – or she – was open to custom. This 'alestake' gradually gave way to a permanent painted sign, but as late as 1594 an alestake is mentioned in Bridport.

The greatest change in brewing took place gradually in the 16th and 17th centuries, when the practice of adding hops to the malted barley became common. The resultant brew was known as 'beer', to distinguish it from 'ale'. The new drink was stronger in flavour but lighter in consistency – and you needed more of it to get drunk. It was cheaper to make because it was reckoned that a bushel of malt would produce eight gallons of ale, but eighteen gallons of beer. It could be stored for longer, and was sold at a slightly cheaper price.

Alehouses were still alehouses, and remained popular. The 'gin-palaces' which invaded London in the early 18th century made little impression in Dorset, even in the ports. Successful brewers sold wholesale to other alehouses, and the practice of 'tied houses' grew up, but the numbers of breweries were still very large even in the 19th century. In 1852 there were fourteen breweries in Sherborne alone.

As in many industries, the arrival of railways revolutionised the distribution of the product. Popular brews went national, and in Dorset brewing became concentrated in major manufactures in the bigger towns. Hall and Woodhouse in Blandford, Devenish in Weymouth, Palmers in Bridport and Eldridge Pope in Dorchester are prime examples.

Brewing was recognised as both an art and a science, and the model made by the employees of the now-defunct Dorchester Brewery demonstrates the complicated process. Very different from the ale-wife with her cauldron in the back kitchen!

The Gangers' Hut
Near Portesham

THERE IS A FOOTPATH from Abbotsbury to Portesham. It was part of the track of the Weymouth to Abbotsbury Railway, a branch line of the Great Western Railway.

One of the few signs that indicate that this was once an active and lively scene of mechanical transport is a little wooden hut halfway along the footpath. It is a ruin – indeed it may fall down soon – but it is a symbol of Victorian enterprise and optimism. The Abbotsbury Branch was built after the great surge of railway construction in the mid-19th century, but its promoters had high hopes of good business and profit. The abundance of iron ore in the hills around Abbotsbury at a time when iron and steel were in huge demand suggested that rapid conveyance to the port of Weymouth, and thence by sea or rail to the foundries of the North, could only return huge dividends. The line would be expected to encourage a growing volume of ordinary business freight and numerous passengers. An extension to Axminster and along the coast was frequently mentioned.

The railway opened in 1885, after many years of struggle to assemble the necessary capital. It was soon apparent that the

expected traffic was not going to materialise: the iron ore was not of the kind required, and the ordinary freight and passenger numbers were just not enough. In 1896 the Abbotsbury Railway Company sold out to the Great Western Railway for £27,000, and the line continued to run until nationalisation. British Railways recognised reality and closed the branch in 1952.

For 67 years the little trains – small locomotives usually pulling a single coach plus the occasional van or wagon – ran back and forth from Abbotsbury to Weymouth, stopping at Portesham, Coryates, Friar Waddon, Upwey, Upwey Junction and Radipole. It was the idyllic country branchline beloved of romantics then and now.

The goods-shed survives at Abbotsbury, complete with loading gauge, but it is used to store farm machinery. Otherwise the gangers' hut, with its little fireplace, calls forth memories of the men who spent their lives maintaining the track. The station platform at Abbotsbury can be seen, but otherwise all is gone.

A Wall-Clock
Blandford Town Museum

TODAY EVERYTHING is dominated by the conception of time. Time is measured in tiny fractions of a second for scientific and sporting purposes, and most of us carry watches which are accurate within seconds for years. Two hundred and fifty years ago most people lived their lives with only the rising and setting of the sun as their measure of time, but the Industrial Revolution rapidly altered that. 'Time is Money' said the men of enterprise!

The development of transport was very significant in the history of timekeeping. The coaches of the Royal Mail ran to a strict schedule, and their timing was based on London time measured by the sun at Greenwich. The trouble was the sun rose earlier to the east of London, and later to the west. Most towns had long-established and traditional methods of establishing local time, usually based on sundials. Accordingly the guards on mail coaches were issued with timepieces set to gain or lose time according to the direction they were taking. Dorchester time was approximately nine minutes behind London.

The arrival of railways brought forth a powerful lobby of hard-headed promoters who had no patience with the cumbersome and often inaccurate calculations necessary for time-adjustment, and pressed hard for standard time across the country. In 1840 Brunel's Great Western Railway took the bull by the horns and set all their station clocks by London time.

There was great local opposition, and two sets of time became

common – Local Time and Railway Time. Sometimes public clocks were given two minute-hands, recording both measures.

Complaints against Railway Time included the view that God had established the time by the sun, and to interfere with it was sacrilegious.

As consciousness of time grew among the population, so clockmakers thrived. Many Dorset towns had more than one, and the skills of both cabinet-making and micro engineering became well-developed. This wall-clock made in Blandford by Robert Hood in 1841 is a fine example.

The battle for localism went on, in spite of the use of the new electric telegraph carried by wires alongside railway lines from Greenwich across the United Kingdom by 1855, giving precise Greenwich Mean Time. An incident in Dorchester in the 1850s illustrated the problem. A civil court case being heard at what is now known as the Old Crown Court was due to start at 10.00am. The judge and the defendant had both arrived by train, but the plaintiff had not appeared. After five minutes, the judge said that since the plaintiff had not turned up, he found for the defendant, and the court rose. The plaintiff then arrived, having used local time, with two minutes in hand. Too late – the judge refused to re-convene and the case had to go to Appeal in London at great further expense.

Finally, in 1880 Parliament established Standard Time for the whole country, and the extra minute hands could be removed.

The Dorset Horn
Dorset County Show

"THE FECUNDITY OF the old Dorset ewe, its hardy nature, and its rent-paying qualities have asserted themselves in most of the counties of England" - thus the Editor of the *Dorset County Chronicle* in 1891.

The Dorset Horn breed had been developed particularly during the 19th century through careful selection, to achieve an animal which could lamb twice a year, provided good meat, and was capable of living on windswept hills. With its great curling horns the sheep was instantly recognisable, and indeed was recognised across the world because a very profitable export trade had been achieved to America and Australia as well as Europe and Asia.

However, this very success had bounced back to threaten the prosperity of the sheep-breeders of Dorset. Foreign farmers were now urging their governments to protect their own developing business by imposing customs duties on imports of sheep. In America Congress had passed the McKinley Tariff in 1890, which taxed imported sheep unless they were certified by breeding associations as of pure breeding stock. The Dorset Horn had no such backing, and British exporters faced ruin as demand for their now expensive product dried up.

Farmers of the Dorset Horn in Somerset were the first to react, and proposed to set up an Association based in Taunton. Dorset farmers reacted in horror – of course the Dorset Horn should be based in Dorset. A war of words conducted in vitriolic meetings and in the press resulted eventually in a settlement, and the Dorset Horn Sheep Breeders' Association with royal patronage was created in Dorchester, where its offices are today.

The breed has diminished in numbers, and Poll-Dorsets – ie Dorset Horns without horns – are more numerous, but they can still be found across the world, and are to be seen every year at the Dorset County Show in Dorchester.

An Eddison Steam Roller at Fordington
Kings Road, Dorchester

FOR THIRTY YEARS there had been steam trains, but they were confined to their tracks. Now in 1870 the Traction Engine had arrived, drawing trains of loaded wagons along the roads from the farms of rural Dorset to the railway. Roads suffered from the huge weight, and the magistrates were forced to establish maximum weights for vehicles crossing bridges as so many of them collapsed.

Francis Eddison (1841 – 1888) came down from Yorkshire to establish a Steam Plough Works at Fordington. The machines were made by manufacturers in the North. A steam plough came as a set: two 12-horsepower traction engines with winding-gear and a wide plough. The crew would station the engines at each end of the field, connect them with ropes, and then wind the plough back and forth across the field. The cost of a set was substantial, and it soon became apparent that the steam plough business could only survive through a system of hire.

Mr Eddison lived in Martinstown, commuting to Dorchester and visiting farmers across the whole county. Most of Eddison's business was done by contracting his company to do the ploughing. The Works thrived, with a basic stock of twelve ploughing sets. Servicing the sets was a major activity, mainly done in the machine shops on the site. The engineering skills required were often not sufficient among the local workforce, and many of the managers and foremen were 'immigrants' from the Midlands and the North. Employment as steam ploughmen was much envied, since they could earn twice the weekly wage of a country labourer. A crew included a foreman, two drivers, a steersman guiding the plough, and a cook. Supporting services included teams of carters bringing water and coal to the ploughing site, because the 'monsters' had enormous hunger and thirst. The Works hooter awoke the whole of Dorchester at 5.45am.

The agricultural depression of the 1880s, caused by the huge importation of American meat and corn, drove down the farmers' profits and they could no longer afford steam ploughing. Nothing daunted, Eddison turned to road-rollers, and it so happened that Dorset County Council took over road maintenance in 1888, and needed to hire equipment. The steam roller was very familiar in the first half of the 20th century and Eddison's Works continued for most of that time. Traction engines continued in use until the steam lorry and then the motor lorry made them redundant.

A single steam roller survives on the playing field at Fordington, a permanent reminder of an exciting episode in the history of the County Town, and a source of enjoyment to young boys who climb all over it.

The Dorchester Foundry Castings
Dorset County Museum

AT THE BOTTOM OF Fordington High Street, adjacent to London Road, is a block of flats with the name 'Lott and Walne Ltd' painted in large letters along the wall.

Thus is remembered the Dorchester Foundry for iron and brass-ware.

Iron was manufactured in the town from its beginnings. Signs of industrial hearths have been found on Roman sites such as the recently-excavated old hospital. Until the development of the blast-furnace in the 16th century ironware for tools, weapons and decoration could only be created by a painful process of heating and hammering with forge and anvil. The blast-furnace, in which a powerful draught of air could create a temperature high enough to turn iron ore into a molten stream, made casting into moulds

possible: and so created the iron foundry which was the precursor of the Industrial Revolution.

There were iron and brass founders in Dorchester at least from the mid-19th century and probably earlier. A thriving business would have followed the great mid-Victorian leap forward in food production, with a huge demand for agricultural machinery from horse-hoes to steam-powered traction engines.

Lott and Walne served the town for a century at least. There was a foundry, a machine shop and a yard, and the noise of hammering and casting must have dominated this corner of the borough. The smoke and the smell would have been equally evident around the premises, but inside the works the scene must have aroused thoughts of Hell: red glowing furnaces, semi-darkness, choking fumes, crashing machines and hoarse shouts. Not that the workers would have thought much about it – the work was hard, serious and exhausting – but compared with agricultural labour, well-paid. Next door was a pub called the Noah's Ark, and it was a standing joke that a hole had been knocked through the wall to improve communication!

The Company made iron carts with sprung wheels for liquid manure and water-spraying, reversible-tine harrows, ploughs, rollers, tubular trussed whippletrees (yes, really), horse-hoes, shepherd huts, lamb-creeps and portable handy knife holders – all these were listed on their advertisements. Around Dorchester is the evidence of their other products such as drain covers, meter-box covers, gates, and lamp posts. Water-wheels were a speciality, and in wartime the firm made hand-grenades.

Lott and Walne staggered on into the 1970s, but now the buildings have been converted into elegant apartments. The Dorset County Museum houses a large selection of their wooden patterns.

Bournemouth Pier
Bournemouth

THE DISCOVERY OF the British seaside as a place for recreation dates from the mid-18th century, but its heyday was late Victorian. The development of Bournemouth from barren heath to thriving and populous resort was rapid in the 19th century whirlwind of economic and social change, as the taste and ability to pay for pleasure percolated through the class-system. What the gentry began with their coastal villas blossomed into a great conurbation, with its major industry attending to the needs of massed holiday-makers.

One of the pleasures of the seaside is cruising in the bay. The problem is – how do you get from the beach to board your vessel while remaining dry-shod? And how do you fare if you are not

Bournemouth Pier, early 20th Century.

very nimble and you have to climb the ship's side?

The answer lay in a pier. Walking out to sea along stout planks several feet above the waves, and then up a short gangway to a comfortable seat on deck or in a saloon was much more attractive.

A pier has many advantages. It is cheaper and easier to build than a quayside, and since it is built on struts the tides and currents find little obstruction, and silt does not build up. Vessels can tie up to it in deep water, without fear of going aground.

The disadvantage is – maintenance. Bournemouth's first pier in 1856 was no more than a short wooden jetty, which was quickly extended to a 1000-foot pier. The problem with rotting wood was met with new cast-iron piles in 1866, but the T-shaped pierhead was destroyed by a storm in 1867, and all the wooden superstructure was wrecked by another in 1876. A new iron pier was built in 1880, and covered shelters and a bandstand added in 1885. Further

extensions created a magnificent feature at the height of the Edwardian seaside vogue.

It is noteworthy that no new piers were built in England after the Great War 1914-1918. The cost of maintenance seemed too high, and perhaps the more sophisticated public did not find the thrill of walking over water quite so attractive. When the Nazis threatened to invade in 1940 Bournemouth Pier was seen as a potential landing place for the Germans, and the structure was broken in two.

Re-opened in 1946, the pier recovered its function and a new theatre was built in 1960, attracting very popular entertainers such as Morecambe and Wise, and the Beatles. A further huge reconstruction took place in 1979-81. In 2006 the Pier was handed over to a commercial company, and there are plans to close the theatre and to create a new adventure centre. The boat trips round the bay will continue…

- 86 -
A Stone Crane
Portland

THE ISLAND AND Royal Manor of Portland has oolitic limestone beds, separated by beds of chert. The whitish-grey limestone makes excellent building material, being both strong and capable of a fine finish. With the arrival of gunpowder in the 16th century it became possible to quarry the stone in large quantities. Convenient to the sea, the stone could be shipped to where it was needed, particularly to the expanding City of London. Hence Portland stone was the choice of Sir Christopher Wren for the re-building of St Paul's after the Great Fire in 1666.

Since the stone trade became so profitable, the technical problem of how to get the material from the quarry to the quayside became acute. A horse-and-cart was severely limited in weight-carrying capacity, and the large blocks so much in demand were too heavy. One answer came in 1826 with the 'Merchants' Railway': a steeply-inclined track with iron rails four feet six inches apart running from Priory Corner on Portland Heights down to the piers at Castletown. It worked by gravity on a continuous chain, with the loaded wagons as they descended pulling up the empties. Where necessary horses were used to complete the process, and the system was so efficient it lasted until 1939. An ordinary railway was built round the eastern side of the Island, and eventually connected with Weymouth.

Quarrying produced huge amounts of waste – stone too coarse for building, which was left in great walls. An important use was found for the rejected material. Even after the defeat of Napoleon in 1815 there was a lingering fear of French resurgence and possible attack. The Royal Navy needed a harbour of refuge for its warships in the long stretch of coast between Portsmouth and Plymouth, and the section of Weymouth Bay next to Portland seemed ideal. A breakwater giving protection against the waves thrown up by a north-easterly wind would complete the harbour, and work began in 1847.

The labour necessary to dig out, convey and lay down the material was provided by building a large prison on the Island to house 1300 convicts. For the first ten years Portland was a staging-post for men sentenced to transportation to Australia, but with the abolition of this disposal the labour force became permanent. The first breakwater took twenty-five years to build. Thirty years after that two further breakwaters were added to complete the enclosed anchorage, and in the early 20th century the naval base became established as the regular headquarters for the Home Fleet.

Portland stone is still much in demand, and is used in many public buildings all over the country. Modern quarrying is rather more sophisticated than shots of gunpowder, and transport is mainly by motor lorry.

A Pile of Hemp
Bridport Museum

A PILE OF HEMP may seem a curious object, but it represents an industry, a town, and a way of life in West Dorset which has all but disappeared. Rope and netmaking were for at least 700 years the mainstay of Bridport, and everywhere in the town can be seen the evidence.

The basis lay in the production of hemp and flax in the hills and valleys of West Dorset. The hemp plant grows up to fifteen feet high. The fibres under the skin of the stem are coarse and eminently suitable for twisting into rope. The softer and finer fibres of flax are better for nets.

Braiding needles.

The yarn is spun by twisting the fibres. Originally this was done using a weighted stick known as a spindle whorl, but from at least the 13th century the spinning-wheel made production much faster. Two or more yarns twisted together made 'twine'.

Ropes were made from a multiple of yarns, and since length was required the process was done on 'ropewalks' up to 300 yards long. The narrow alleys of the main streets were very suitable for this. The yarn was attached to revolving hooks at either end, which would be turned with handles, twisting the yarn into rope. To prevent sagging over the great length, supports known as 'skirders' were used, with vertical pegs to separate the yarns. Thus were the ropes made for fishing boats, merchant ships and battleships from the 13th to the 20th centuries. Nelson's *Victory* used about twelve miles of rope.

Nets were made from flax by hand, using wooden braiding needles which could carry a length of twine to be paid out as the knitter tied the knots used to keep the net together. This work was done by both men and women: though it was not unusual for a man and his son to be making the rope in the street while the mother and daughter made the nets in the kitchen.

In Victorian times the demand for rope and nets was great enough for huge sheds to be built to house the ropewalks, with net-fitting carried on in the lofts. Gradually the individual businesses amalgamated. As sail gave way to steam, demand for rope diminished, and the industry adapted to meet other needs, such as nets for different kinds of sport. Man-made fibres eclipsed hemp and flax, and worldwide competition gradually reduced production in Bridport to a trickle.

- 88 -
The Penny-Farthing Bicycle
The Priest's House Museum, Wimborne

WALKING WAS THE only means of local travel for most people until the late Victorian period. By 1900 the bicycle had begun a transport revolution, for work and pleasure. Getting about on two wheels had been an interest for inventors from the beginning of the 19th century. Until the 1860s this had mainly consisted of sitting astride a wooden frame with a wheel in front and a wheel behind, with the rider 'paddling' to get motion. Considerable speeds could be achieved especially downhill, but the equipment was expensive.

A French adaptation in 1863 put cranks and pedals on the front wheel to create the 'Velocipede', but metal tyres and rough roads did not give comfort, and top speed was limited. These wooden bicycles were popularly known as 'Boneshakers'.

A decade later came the 'High Wheel' cycle, which also gained a popular name as the 'Penny-Farthing'. The front wheel was huge, the rear one was small. The rider sat high and pedalled direct as for the Velocipede, but the diameter of the wheel meant that the ground covered for each turn was far greater, and much higher speeds could be attained. The ride was more comfortable, the tyres were hard

rubber and with advances in technology the frame could be made of light tubular steel. The wheel spokes were of thin metal wire. However, steering was cumbersome, and the machine very dangerous.

The problem lay in the riding position. When the great wheel hit even a small obstruction in the road it would stop dead and the rider would literally 'take a header' over the handlebars. Cycling tended to be restricted to young men willing to take a risk!

The 'Penny-Farthing' was the bicycle of the 1870s. In 1883 came the 'Safety' bicycle, which was the basis of all future designs. The wheels were of equal size, the pedals and cranks were separate and the power was taken to the rear wheel with a chain. Dunlop introduced the pneumatic rubber tyre in 1886. Within a few years cycling for men and women became very popular, as relatively cheap transport and as recreation. With bikes came popular engineering.

Dorset people in town and country took to cycling in a big way. Cycle shops sprang up to give sales and service. In Dorchester in the 1890s Mr Tilley not only had a shop but gave bicycle lessons to young ladies along the tree-lined 'Walks'.

- 89 and 90 -
"Secundus" Clay Railway Locomotive
Norden Railway Museum
And a Clay Basket
Poole Museum

CLAY IS NOT OBVIOUSLY very attractive or valuable: but Purbeck Blue Clay or ball-clay is different, and for 250 years it has been a highly-regarded and substantial part of the Dorset economy. Why *ball* clay? The most likely derivation is that when handled it forms easily into balls.

The great property of ball-clay is that it turns from a bluish tinge to a brilliant white in the potter's kiln. It is also very strong and can produce thin china-ware. Smoking tobacco in pipes began in England in the late 16th century, and ball-clay was ideal for making such pipes. Mining developed, and then came the surge in pottery associated with the name of Wedgwood.

In 1771 Josiah Wedgwood ordered 1400 tons of ball-clay from the landowner and Poole businessman Thomas Hyde of Arne. Soon clay-mines were being dug in other parts of Purbeck, and by 1796 half the male population of Corfe were clay-cutters.

Transport of the raw material to the potteries in the Midlands was by coastal craft and then canal. Goathom Pier was constructed – but carriage across Purbeck was slow and clumsy without good roads. In the 19th century narrow-gauge tramways were built, with horse-drawn wagons, but steam was the answer and locomotives were constructed. As its name suggests 'Secundus' was the second in a series of such engines. Built in 1874 it served until the line was abandoned in 1955.

After several attempts a standard-gauge railway was opened from Wareham to Swanage in 1885, thus making a connection to the whole country. As production greatly increased to meet national and international demand, two main companies emerged: Pikes and Fayles. These finally joined together in 1949 and were taken over by English China Clays in 1964. By the late 20th century production was running at 150,000 tons a year.

The tramways and the Swanage Railway closed as road transport took over. The export of ball-clay (banned by Parliament from 1662 to 1853) has flourished. It is estimated that 50% of the world's sanitary ware contains ball-clay from the United Kingdom. It is our secondmost important mineral export after oil.

'Secundus' Locomotive.

Thomas Hardy's Study
Dorset County Museum

THOMAS HARDY SITS stonily at Top-o-Town Dorchester and reflects on the passing scene. Most people don't even notice the statue, and literate tourists on pilgrimage to Casterbridge have to be directed to it. Of course it is the novelist and poet, his life-long association with Dorchester and the fictional name of Casterbridge that he bestowed on it, that visitors and inhabitants alike think of first.

Thomas Hardy was born in 1840 in Bockhampton, a hamlet just east of Dorchester. The cottage, owned by the National Trust, is open to visitors. His family lived modestly but found the money to pay for his education, and he walked several miles to school in the town. Eventually he trained as an architect in an office in South Street, but gradually turned to writing novels and poetry: the novels to bring in enough money to support the poet. And they did – the novels were very widely popular in the early 20th century.

Hardy's theme was life in 'Wessex' in the early and middle years of the 19th century: a culture that was fast disappearing as he wrote. 'Wessex' was loosely Dorset, and the placenames he made up are clearly related to actual towns and villages. The description of 'Casterbridge' in the novel *The Mayor of Casterbridge* is evocative of Dorchester as Hardy remembered it from his childhood and in its undeveloped days before the railway – though only just.

Two particular themes dominate his work: first there is Nature and the special environment of the Wessex countryside, and second the characters of the inhabitants.

Nature is portrayed as inexorable. The brooding hills, the grim Egdon Heath, the darkness of woods – all bear down on the people struggling to make a living and to deal with relationships. Tragedy strikes without warning.

Hardy is particularly effective in his adumbration of the characters of stronger women, such as 'Tess of the Durbervilles', and Eustacia Vye in *Return of the Native*. In the hardships of 19th century country life he had clearly known such women personally.

A wide variety of male characters are vigorously described: stout farmers, poor rustics and plausible rogues, all fighting for their places in the unconquerable scheme of Nature and unrelenting Fate.

A sense of History comes through in much of his writing, especially in *The Trumpet Major,* a story about the Invasion Crisis of 1803. It is curiously evocative of the scene in 1940, twelve years after the novelist's death in 1928.

Long-term families in Dorchester have traditional stories about Thomas Hardy in the community. Most of the stories are not very complimentary: he was remembered living grouchily in his house at Max Gate. One old railwayman told his daughter how Hardy had ordered him to get off his bike and walk with his dog.

In the Dorset County Museum there is a section devoted to Hardy, which includes not only a substantial collection of his papers and memorabilia but a full-size reconstruction of the study at Max Gate with its original furniture. It is atmospheric.

A Traditional School Desk
Dorset County Museum

THE WOODEN DESK with hinged lid and ceramic ink-well is a symbol of education as it developed for children in the 19th and 20th centuries. There were different designs: some had sloping tops, some were had seats attached on metal frames, some were fixed in pairs, some had shelves rather than boxes for books. Most were badly treated in spite of dire threats, and had ink-stains, carved initials and rude drawings before being scrapped when joints finally gave way.

The ink-well was a sign of progress in writing, and the transition from slate and pencil to paper with pen and ink was often painful – literally if carelessness with ink was punished. The ink was made in school by dissolving powder in water in a large stone jar, which was then carried from desk to desk to fill the ink-wells. The pen was a painted wooden stick with a metal slot into which a replaceable nib was fitted. When dipped it would retain enough ink for a few words. If overdipped, drops of ink would form blots which had then to be dried with absorbent blotting-paper, which had also to be applied to writing to prevent smearing. Today's children have no idea how their forebears suffered!

Thomas Hardy the writer walked three miles to school in Dorchester, attending the private school of Mr Last, a Nonconformist minister. His parents found the fees, even though they were plain country folk with little to spare.

The demands of the Industrial Revolution in commerce and technology inspired a great advance in mass education. Among better-off people there was a strong feeling that the lower classes should be taught the principles of religion, and should be able to read the Scriptures. The National Society, a Church of England charity founded in 1811, set up schools in towns and villages across the country, with small fees and providing basic education.

From the 1830s onwards the government took an increasing interest in education, gradually increasing subsidies to the educational charities. In 1870 local School Boards were set up to ensure that elementary tuition was available to all, and attendance to the age of 10 was made compulsory from 1880, and free in 1890. Local Education Authorities (mainly County Councils) were instituted in 1902. Part of their duty was to set up secondary education for suitable children – though this did not become free until 1944.

Before 1800 literacy was scarce among country children, and not very frequent in towns. Education had to be paid for: from the humble 'Dame-school', where a single woman acted as a child-minder and taught some to read, to the ancient foundations where boys studied a classical curriculum in preparation for the professions.

The age for compulsory attendance was raised to 14 in 1918, 15 in 1947 and 16 in 1972. There are proposals to raise it yet again to 18.

A School Logbook
Dorset History Centre

IN THE VICTORIAN Age the United Kingdom Government gradually took a greater part in financing and controlling the education of children. For a long time this consisted of making grants to schools run by Voluntary Societies, mainly religious. Inspectors checked to see the money was properly spent and from 1862 the size of the grant was determined by the success of the school as tested by the Inspector. In supportive evidence the schools were required to keep Logbooks, recording all important activities and events.

Logbooks were kept for eighty years, and exist today in Record Offices to give insight not just into education but into many aspects of social life in town and country.

Martinstown School, now a private house.

A Logbook for Martinstown School, four miles south-west of Dorchester, begins in December 1895 with an entry saying that the Infants had been issued with new slates. Attendance was a matter of great importance, recorded in the registers but frequently the subject of comment and explanation in the Logbook. Low attendance might be due to severe weather such as storms or heavy snowfall – children from outlying farms walked miles to school. Epidemics of measles and whooping cough seem to have occurred often, and in the winter of 1901-2 the school was closed for seven weeks. Haymaking and harvest meant that the labour of older children was required, no doubt to their pleasure. There were several occasions in the course of the year when the school was regularly closed: the building was used for the collection of annual rents by the agent of the Lord of the Manor, and at Martinstown Fair in November the children had an extra two-and-a-half days holiday.

There were two classrooms and a staff of one Head Teacher and an Assistant. The Assistant was often untrained, and known as a Pupil-teacher. In 1904 the Assistant was a recent pupil at the school, and normally taught the Infants – the Inspectors suggested that she should spend part of her week at the Infants' School in Dorchester to see how it was done.

In that same year of 1904 a new Head Teacher was appointed and recorded her great dissatisfaction in the state of the school. The premises were badly maintained, and the children had dirty habits and displayed a singular lack of intelligence! Miss Pritchard had a difficult time, not least with the Assistant who after one altercation took a copy of the School Rules and burnt them in front of her. The Police came to the school to complain that children had been throwing stones at passing motor-cars, and the older boys took time off to see the pig-killing. Miss Pritchard retired early.

1896 Ap. 2nd Broke up for Easter
holiday one week. The school was
used as a polling station on Monday
from 12 to 8 so there was no sch. in
the afternoon. Ar. for the week 50.1

Ap 17th Held school again this week.
Have admitted some children in
place of those who left the village
at Lady-day. Ordinary work
& progress.   The 6 children
who were examined for labour
certificates 5 passed in all
subjects 1 failed in spelling

24th Have admitted some more children
in place of those who have left the
village. The attendance has been
fairly good. Mr Brown called
on Friday, but with one exception
he could not take names.
Stds I & II & III have had the Cat and
the Dog as object Lessons this week

Copy of H. M. I s Report-

" The order is fairly good and the
School has made very fair progress
in the Elementary Subjects. English
has improved and is now fair, while
Needlework Recitation and Singing
are creditable. Efficient help for
the Infants class should be provided
at once and so should the desk,
cupboard, and urinal for infant boys,
all of which were asked for last year"
The attention of the Managers is
requested to the last paragraph of
Article 85 (b) of the Code and the last
paragraph of Article 101 (b) i.
Have found the above correct.
Arthur Symonds
Corresp. Manager

A Bournemouth Tramcar
The Museum of Electricity, Christchurch

THE HEY-DAY OF local public transport was the first half of the 20th century, and peak usage in south-east Dorset was the year 1950.

The advent of electrical power late in Victoria's reign made town tramways practical, and the internal-combustion engine replaced the horses for buses. The rise in real wages meant travel was more affordable, and commuting to work more widespread, but then after World War Two the rapid spread of personal motoring reduced demand for public transport.

The first proposal for a privately-owned 'light railway' from the station at Bournemouth Central to Poole was made in 1881, but this was opposed by both town Corporations who wanted control of such a radical change. In 1901 the company known as Poole and District Electric Tramways opened their first line from Poole Station to County Gates, with a fleet of 17 tramcars powered by overhead wires. The following year Bournemouth Corporation began the creation of a network of services centred on The Square and radiating to Winton in the north, Poole in the west and Christchurch in the east. For a few years the central section was powered by underground conduits to assuage complaints of unsightliness, but in 1911 this was converted to overhead wires.

In 1905 Poole Corporation bought the Poole and District Tramways, and promptly leased the business to Bournemouth for thirty years. This established a formidable system of town public transport, with tramcars painted in a livery of chocolate and primrose-yellow, and a staff of inspectors clothed in what was described as 'gorgeous apparel' which closely resembled the uniform of a military staff officer. The power for the system was generated by a coal-fired station in Southcote Road.

At first no Sunday services were allowed, in face of opposition from churchmen. This was relaxed in 1913 for Sunday afternoons and in 1926 for the whole day.

Gradually motor buses took over more and more of the traffic, and in an effort to compete the Corporation dug up all the tramlines in 1936 and replaced the trams with trolleybuses – still using the overhead wires but running on rubber tyres. They too finally disappeared in 1969, leaving the field free for the ubiquitous motor-bus.

Trams are still remembered with affection, and Number 85 has pride of place in the Museum of Electricity. Recently a Bournemouth MP has renewed a suggestion that a tramway should be built from Bournemouth Airport to the beach, with park-and-ride stops on the way. The day of the tram is not quite done!

The Baden-Powell Memorial
Brownsea Island, Poole

SCOUTING WAS A phenomenon of the 20th century, and it continues to progress. It was the conception of one man, whose charisma and organising ability are commemorated in the memorial stone set up where Scouting began.

Robert Baden-Powell was a senior army officer who had distinguished himself during the Siege of Mafeking in the Boer War in 1899. His experiences, together with a strong awareness of the needs of young men, convinced him that organised outdoor training combined with promotion of high principles would go far to help the social problems of the time.

In retirement he devoted himself to thinking, speaking and writing about this. He came up with a plan to hold an experimental camp for a group of twenty boys from different backgrounds, where he could try out his ideas. The camp took place on Brownsea Island in Poole Harbour in August 1907, with boys from Eton and Harrow public schools together with less-privileged boys from Poole and Bournemouth.

The camp seems to have been a great success, and in January 1908 Baden-Powell published *Scouting for Boys*. The book was to become the 'bible' for scouting, and it inspired the formation of Boy Scout Troops across the country and eventually the world.

Scouting was based on elements of military discipline, with aims of goodwill, responsibility and service all bonded together with enjoyment and comradeship. It was a magic mix which appealed particularly to boys – and later girls – from the upper working-class and lower middle-class, though it spread throughout the community.

The Scout uniform began at Brownsea with a khaki scarf, a brass fleur-de-lys badge and a coloured shoulder knot to identify the wearer's 'Patrol', or section. Baden-Powell had recognised the need of boys to 'belong', and used it for 'good' purposes in competitive activities far removed from the anti-social activities of street gangs.

Soon after Scouting began, a well-wisher donated Gilwell Park in Hertfordshire to the Movement, and a local boy met Baden-

Powell there. Don Potter became a wood-carver and sculptor in later life, and they remained friends. Potter taught at Bryanston School in Dorset for forty-one years, and in 1967 sculpted the Memorial Stone to commemorate the 60th anniversary of the beginning of Scouting on Brownsea.

A World War One Tank
Bovington Tank Museum

THERE ARE MANY military sites along the south coast of England: entirely to be expected when any attack was likely to come across the Channel. Suitable terrain for army manoeuvres was always in demand and thus the heathland around Bovington seemed entirely appropriate for a camp where exercises and rifle practice might be carried out. The war that inspired the move was very distant – it was the Boer War in South Africa in 1899.

Seventeen years later, in the midst of a very different and much closer war, Bovington was chosen for the development of an entirely new weapon – the tank.

Soon after the outset of World War One, it became apparent that the combination of defensive trenches and massed machine guns had created stalemate on the Western Front. Attackers would suffer huge casualties, and the traditional fast movers on the battlefield, the cavalry, could not move at all through the mud.

Mechanical devices were anathema to the generals, and in 1915 Winston Churchill pressed the Royal Navy to develop 'land ships'. Experiments were made with armoured vehicles with caterpillar tracks, propelled by internal combustion engines. Secrecy resulted in the name 'tank' being applied, the crates being labelled 'water-tanks'. Training and manoeuvres took place at Bovington. Early trials were often failures as the technology lagged behind the demands, but in September 1916 the first tanks were employed on the Front.

The assumption had been that tanks would operate in support of infantry, moving up with them in attack on the enemy trenches. It was indeed a shock to the Germans, but the rate of mechanical failure was very high, and German infantry soon learned the weaknesses.

Eventually the British were able to mass 400 tanks for a crushing blow on the German line at Cambrai in November 1917. It was successful, but the infantry failed to follow up and exploit the gains. In April 1918 occurred the first tank versus tank battle – three British Mark IVs versus one enormous German A7V. It was inconclusive – all were damaged.

At Amiens on August 8th 1918, the first great victory for the tank was achieved when 600 lumbering monsters crashed through the German line, creating what the German General Von Ludendorff called 'the Black Day of the German Army'.

German surrender in November 1918 meant hundreds of tanks were redundant. Those not wrecked were shipped back to Bovington for storage and repair. Bovington became the headquarters of the Royal Tank Regiment. After World War Two the Tank Museum was developed for the instruction and pleasure of multitudes of visitors.

The War Memorial at Bryants Puddle
Bryants Puddle Village

RICH AND POWERFUL men sometimes develop an urge to build an ideal community. In Dorset Milton Abbas, Poundbury and Bryants Puddle are good examples.

Early in the 20th century Ernest Debenham was rich in the family business of retail drapery. In 1914 he bought part of the estate of the Framptons of Moreton, and his purchase included the hamlet of Bryants Puddle. Debenham determined to create a thriving farming community based on scientific principles and social concern.

Bryants Puddle Centre.

The Great War 1914-1918 interrupted initial progress, but in the 1920s he pursued his ideas with vigour. Debenham believed that by applying the methods of science and business in an efficient manner dairy-farming could be revolutionised and would not only produce great profits but would greatly increase employment.

To house the new work-force forty new cottages were built to add to the original twelve of the hamlet. The new houses were to have inside toilets and each would have at least a quarter of an acre of garden. Bladen Farm was to be the centre of crop production, and the dairy was based at Milborne St Andrew. At its height there were 600 workers on the estate of 10,000 acres.

The importance of good transport was recognised in the Depot which looked after two heavy steam wagons, sixteen tractors and numerous lorries, vans and cars. Electrical power was created with two oil-fired generators at Bridge House, and a good water-supply was provided by a pumping station and borehole.

Experiments were wide-ranging: mass production of eggs, selective breeding of animals, forestry and beekeeping were all given attention. The dairy at 'The Ring' was the first to have a large-scale system of milking machines in Dorset. For ten years from 1919 to 1929 the whirlwind of change continued, until the Depression dried up the source of money to be invested. The estate was never self-supporting, but the ideas and achievements proved valuable to the farming industry in time to come, and in recognition Ernest Debenham was knighted in 1931.

Gradually the impetus diminished, the farms were let, and when Debenham died in 1952 the estate was broken up.

An early enterprise had been the village War Memorial, sculpted by the famous Eric Gill, and begun in typical Debenham vigour almost a year before the end of the Great War.

A Home Guard Armband
Military Museum, Dorchester

THIS IS A VERY SMALL object to represent a significant element of wartime life in Dorset. The sudden German Blitzkrieg in April and May 1940 resulted in the British Expeditionary Force being driven out of France via the beaches at Dunkirk. The British Government anticipated the possibility of German invasion, and on 14th May appealed for civilian men to join the Local Defence Volunteers.

This continued a tradition in Dorset which could be traced back through the Napoleonic invasion scares to the Armada preparations, and eventually back to the Anglo-Saxon *Fyrd*.

Huge numbers aged 17 to 60 came forward, but of course neither uniforms nor weapons were available. At first, there were only armbands inscribed LDV, but the name of the force was soon changed to 'Home Guard'. In Dorset, as 150 years earlier, weapons depended on local initiative, with shotguns from the farmers and sportsmen, and all kinds of edged and pointed equipment. Ancient collections of pikes and cutlasses were raided, and basic drills attempted.

If Hitler had managed to land an invasion force in the summer and autumn of 1940, there is little doubt that the German Army, strongly equipped, fresh from conquest and effectively led, would have found the Home Guard no more than a passing irritation; and the Regular British Army had not had time to re-organise after their retreat across the Channel.

The extraordinary thing is that no-one seems to have realised this – or if they did, they kept quiet. Winston Churchill's rhetoric, relayed by the BBC, stimulated the conviction that the Germans would be torn apart in the streets and lanes of England.

Meanwhile, the Nazis were planning to destroy the Royal Air Force before comfortably cruising over. Everybody knows they failed, as the RAF won the Battle of Britain, and Hitler first postponed and then cancelled the invasion. Warmwell Aerodrome near Dorchester housed a squadron of Spitfires which played a significant part in this.

While that was going on, the Home Guard was being developed as a proper force. Uniforms were issued, rifles acquired from America, and training programmes organised with the co-operation of the Regular Army. In the end, over a million men enlisted – and were gathered into platoons, companies and battalions. By October 1940 Bournemouth, Poole and Boscombe each registered a battalion of 2,500 men. Dorchester had a company of 200. Many of the older men had served in World War One, and thus provided a solid backbone. They were never needed – but what a magnificent response.

Dorset was a potential invasion area, and links between the local military bases and the Home Guard were established. Across the county there are still old men – young boys in 1940 – who served in 'Dad's Army'.

- 99 -
The Dorset WI World War Two Record Book 1939-1945
Dorset History Centre

JUST AFTER THE end of the Second World War the Dorset Federation of Women's Institutes decided to compile a manuscript volume of members' recollections of their activities during the War. The result was a substantial document which was filed away and eventually presented to the County Record Office. Some years ago the significance of the volume was recognized when it was declared to be a 'National Treasure' by the British Library, and it was publicised nationwide.

The Women's Institute Movement began in Canada in the 1890s and the first British one was formed in 1915. The date is important: one of the triggers was the need to encourage countrywomen to take part in the Great War by helping in the production and efficient use of food. Each Institute is a local club in which women of all backgrounds come together for fellowship, mutual understanding and education. The social mix is very important. Until the early 20th century the class differences were so enormous that an all-encompassing association would have been impossible, but the advance in state education and improving living conditions had begun to break class-barriers.

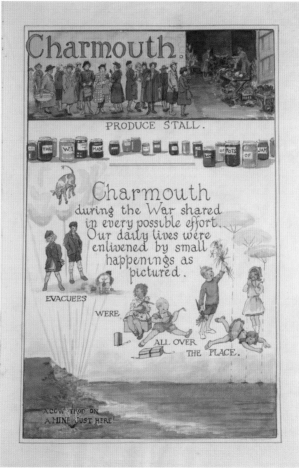

By the beginning of World War Two there were several thousand Institutes in Britain, serving their communities and beginning to flex their muscles in the direction of the improvement of women's rights throughout society. The War provided an enormous opportunity for public service and the WI set to with a will.

All kinds of activity are recorded in the returns made after the War by no fewer than 83 Dorset Institutes: help given to refugees, the collection of clothes for bomb-damage victims, care for children evacuated from large cities, the mass production of jam and rose-hip syrup (the latter a valuable substitute for unobtainable oranges and vitamin C) – and much else. Among the most extraordinary entries is that of Portland WI whose service was vital in the care for 10,000 French and Moroccan troops who had escaped from the German conquest of France in 1940.

The reports vary from the purely factual details to elaborately illustrated and humorous accounts. All go to show how the communities were welded together in the face of extreme danger and mounting hardship. The War Book is indeed a significant object in the History of Dorset.

The American War Memorial
Weymouth Esplanade

IN THE EARLY summer of 1944 much of Dorset was an armed camp. The enormous – and secret – preparations for the liberation of Europe from the Nazis were in their final stages.

From Devon through Dorset and Hampshire to Sussex, British and American invasion forces were organised to leave from various ports, planning to join together in one massive assault on the Normandy beaches. In advance of the seaborne landing, airborne troops landing by parachute and glider would create havoc behind the defences and seize vital bridgeheads.

It would be the greatest seaborne invasion in the History of the World.

From Weymouth, Portland and Poole were to come the American Army V Corps. The US First Infantry 1Division – the 'Big Red One' – were to make the assault on 'Omaha' Beach. The troops were in camps all over Dorset: large camps like those at Blandford and Sherborne, and smaller ones in many villages. The huge American lorries, full of laughing, cigar-smoking and gum-chewing GIs rumbled and crashed through Dorset lanes, often followed by Sherman tanks tearing up road surfaces.

As D-day approached South Dorset was shut down, with strict movement controls. The cheerful badinage between soldiers and villagers became more restricted. In early June the infantry embarked on the landing craft at Weymouth Quay, the tanks in Portland harbour.

At Tarrant Rushton airfield the airborne troops waited by their gliders, setting off in the night of 5th/6th June. The British forces sailed from Southampton, Portsmouth and Shoreham, and the rest of the Americans from Devon. The huge armada assembled off Normandy.

The attack on Omaha Beach proved to be the most difficult of all, meeting fierce German resistance. A thousand of those GIs who had been joking with the Dorset girls a few days earlier were killed on the first landing, and many thousands injured. The Memorial to the American dead was put up on Weymouth Esplanade in 1947.

- 101 -
The Fountain at Poundbury
Poundbury, Dorchester

UNTIL THE LATE 19th century Dorchester was still largely confined within its Roman wall – though the wall itself had fallen long before. There was great demand for expansion, fuelled by the railway, the brewery and the new County Council administration – but Dorchester was surrounded by the 3000 acres of the Duchy of Cornwall, and George Herriot, the Steward from 1865 until 1899, was reluctant to make any land available. He particularly disliked the proposals for cheaper housing, though at the time the only such housing in Dorchester was the slum area of Mill Street, Fordington.

Some large villas had been built along Prince of Wales Road in the 1880s, but it was not until after the departure of Herriot that Victoria Park was developed for working class houses, helped by greater economic confidence before the Great War. Slow progress in the '20s and '30s was interrupted by World War Two. Even after 1945 when there was considerable pressure for country towns to take some of the overspill from war-torn London and Bristol, the Duchy policy was to hold back on the further disposal of farming land.

In 1969 Prince Charles came of age and as Duke of Cornwall took charge of the estates which provided the income for the heir to the throne. For the first time in centuries the Duchy was headed by a man whose interests lay in culture and society as well as in 'country pursuits'.

Gradually his ideas developed, and in the 1980s he began to speak publicly about his dislike of some aspects of modern architecture and town-design. The stark tower-blocks and sprawling suburbia which had proliferated to meet the demand for housing were criticised as 'sheer unadulterated ugliness and mediocrity' in the Prince's book *A Vision for Britain* in 1988.

Discussions with planners and architects resulted in a new concept of a pedestrian-friendly and attractive urban area in which an amalgam of classical designs, varied social communities, industrial and commercial enterprises and cultural amenities, would make a valuable and appreciated extension to Dorchester. The consultant Leon Krier held wide public consultations, in which the aim of creating something akin to an Italian hilltop village was explained. Inevitably there was some local disquiet, but suggestions were absorbed and the building of Poundbury on the western outskirts of Dorchester commenced in 1993.

Twenty years on, with Phase Two nearing completion, and two more phases to go, can it be said that the Prince's aims have been achieved? With some reservations the answer is probably 'yes'. The car is still universal, but not to the fore, and there are no racetracks. The visual aspects are generally pleasing, and approaching from the west Poundbury even looks something like an Italian hilltop town. Industry is not very significant, and the social mix is overwhelmingly middle-class and middle-aged. Most inhabitants are pleased to live there. Old Dorchester is becoming used to its western extension – slowly.

The fountain near the chocolate factory is a fitting object, representing some of the aspirations of His Royal Highness.

Poundbury.